Don't Blame The Road

Copyright © 2006, 2020 Rose Bilal. All rights reserved. This book may not be reproduced in whole or in part without written permission from the publisher, except by a reviewer who may quote brief passages in a review; nor may any part of this book be reproduced, stored in retrieval system, or transmitted in any form or by any means, electronic, mechanical, photocopying, recording, or other, without prior written permission from the publisher.

ISBN-13: 978-1-7358398-2-0 Paperback
ISBN-13: 978-1-7358398-3-7 eBook
Printed and bound in the United States of America
November 2020

Published by
Sula Too Publishing
Tampa, Florida
www.sulatoo.com/publishing

Don't Blame The Road

Navigating Through Life
Discovering Your Innate Abilities

By Rose Bilal

Sula Too Publishing
Tampa Florida

This book is dedicated To

*to the memory of my sister,
Annette Peeler*

Contents

Foreword	9
Chapter 1 - Welcome To The Road	11
Chapter 2 - Questionable Lane Change	23
Chapter 3 - Shining Headlights Straight Ahead	31
Chapter 4 - Moving in Reverse	49
Chapter 5 - Road Under Construction	69
Chapter 6 - Flat Tire Blues	79
Chapter 7 - One Way Out	87
Chapter 8 - Shifting Gears	95
Chapter 9 - Tootin' The Horn	101
Chapter 10 - Caution: Soft Shoulders	105
Chapter 11 - Smoothing Out A Bumpy Road	113
Chapter 12 - Navigating Reality	119
Chapter 13 - My Turn Signals Are Working!	127
Chapter 14 - Nearing My Destination	135
Chapter 15 - Smooth Road Ahead	145
Chapter 16 - Bless The Road	151

Author's note

I have changed the names of some of the people who appear in my story. This has been done because it is not my intention to offend anyone, but simply to tell the truth as I know it.

Inspritation For Title of This Book

While stuck in interstate traffic, I was intrigued by the radio DJ deep voice reporting on the accident causing the backup. He was explaining with hard core conviction that the terrible accident was the result of bad road conditions.

At that instant a vivid picture of how I viewed the world begin to play out on the screen of my consciousness. I clearly saw words which read; WHY BLAME THE ROAD? If we recognize hazardous, unsafe conditions why don't we act responsibly and slow down.

It was then that I realized how my life was like the road. And that I had been blaming others for the "wrong way" I was driving on it.

For bookings, CDs or commissions: rsbilal@aol.com or (813) 221-3088

Acknowledgments

I first want to thank Dr. M. Tina Dupree, "The Chicken Lady," for inspiring me to put my life experiences into words. Thanks to Robert and Penny for being a loving force in my life. I also thank my very good friend, Patricia "Trish" Gullett, for having the patience of Job while showing me what it takes to become a writer. I thank my godmother, Bunmi, for connecting me to Orisha and the spirit world of my ancestors. I want to thank my best friend and "sister," Vertyle Moss, for her unconditional love and support; and for believing in me when nobody else did.

Thanks, gratitude, and love to the late Al Downing and Mr. Ernie Calhoun for giving me the opportunity to sharpen my vocal skills with your jazz band, and for being good and loyal friends. My deepest thanks to Dr. Michael Walker, a good friend, fellow actor, and the best dentist in the Tampa Bay Area. My sincere and heartfelt thanks to Aubrey and Susan Hampton for making it possible to keep my dream alive. Thank you, Anna Brennen, for teaching me about the inner world of theater and the art of acting. Thanks, Mom, for giving me life. Thanks to Holly Hardin, Turk Nelson, and Mary Marshall for sharing your home with me when I was homeless. You're the best friends in the world.

Thanks to Nancie Bridges for helping me understand the language of the computer. Thank you, Debbie "Happy" Cohen, for sharing your time and business knowledge. My sincere thanks to my book editor and writing coach Willy Mathis, for everything! Thanks to all my fellow visual artists who continue to offer their help and support whenever I need their expertise: Oliver Parsons, Debbie Rodriguez, Jerry Robinson, Kenneth Dickerson, and Ron Berman. To all the talented musicians I've had the privilege of working with-you know who you are-thanks for making me sound so great! To Bobby Garcia, Roy "Turk" Nelson and Nathan Page, thanks for filling my soul with beautiful musical memories.

I am grateful for all the people who took precious time to read my manuscript and give their helpful feedback: Anna Brennen, Gary Monroe, Vee Williams, Bunny Downing, Peggy Sinclair, Anita Shumway, Dave and Dawn Snider, Nathan Burton, Kevin Wilder, Glenda "GiGi" Lewis, Larry Younger, Malcolm Johnson, Aline Campbell, Al and Geri McDaniel, Fran Powers, Nancy Dalence, Shelaine Peters, Elizabeth Bettendorf, and Maureen Van Trease. To anyone whose name I failed to mention, please know that I am forever grateful for your support.

"Rose Bilal has written a story of resilience and hope for girls and women, especially those whose lives and spirits may have been damaged by abuse, neglect or emotional abandonment. Rose has emerged as a "phoenix from the ashes" with her remarkable talents and creativity now defining her and her future. Rose's message to girls is powerful and positive, the essence of our community initiative for girls in Tampa. "
Liz Kennedy, Founder Ophelia Project-Tampa Bay

"A compelling story about life's journey. The cycle of abuse can be broken. Rose Bilal has reached another milestone."
Angeleah Kinsler/Director of Human Resources The Child Abuse Council

"As a black citizen I adore you; as a law enforcement officer I certainly applaud you. You did not have to divulge your past because I am sure most had no idea. But rest assured I am positive by doing so, somewhere you have not inspired not just one life, but many."
Robert C. Oates, Major (retired)District I enforcement Operations Department

"Rose Bilal's memoir was written with introspective candor and represents the last leg of her journey to become whole as a person."
Gary Monroe, author, The Highwaymen and Extraordinary Interpretations

"With her stunning autobiography, Rose Bilal reveals the struggles and triumphs of a girl-child and young woman, whose gained wisdom has informed her journey as an adult actress, vocalist, visual artist, motivational speaker and author. Don't' Blame The Road is a courageous, richly told story that is also poignant, poetic, at times deliciously funny, and always engrossing. "

Vee Williams Garcia, author, The Jazz Flower

Foreword

I've known Rose Bilal as a jazz singer, actress and visual artist. She's a woman who doesn't believe in creative boundaries and always pours vivid, life-affirming colors into her art, her acting and her singing.

What I didn't learn until reading this book is the long, difficult road she traveled to reach success both as an artist and a human being. From the start, "Don't Blame The Road" tells the story of a woman who faced seemingly every adversity and challenge life could hand out. I won't run through a list of those challenges here. Rose does that so much better in her own words. But I'm reminded of all the movies that have been made about women overcoming adversity. Rose's story contains enough adversity and enough overcoming for a dozen film biographies.

What strikes me so much about Rose's story is how she always found a way to reinvent herself when times were darkest. She retains an optimism that would have been dashed in a lesser person. She also takes the reader vividly into the world of 1960s rhythm and blues bands at a time when some of the greatest music of the 20th century was being made.

Enjoy Rose's story and, after that, go see her perform. Her life story is in these pages, but it's also in every note she sings, every character she portrays and every piece of art she creates.

Paul Wilborn
Creative Industries Manger
City of Tampa

Chapter 1

Welcome To The Road
"Early Years"

December 10, 1947. We'd moved into our new apartment just a few weeks before and I didn't like it there. I wondered if all the houses in Newark, New Jersey, were the same – dark, even with the lights on. A scary old round stove stood prominently in the middle of the room where we were sitting. The rug was all torn up and it smelled like old bacon grease.

My brother Bobby said that my mom had prayed to heaven and asked the angels to find us a place we could afford. I answered that I didn't know why she would have asked for the rag-stuffed cracks in the windows but I guessed they came with the free furniture.

Seven-year-old Bobby, who prided himself on knowing everything, said I was the dumbest person he ever met. Since I was only five and he was the oldest and a boy, I knew he must be right. My brother called me stupid so often that I thought only boys were allowed by God to be smart.

Bobby never wanted me hanging around and, yet, wouldn't try to make friends with the boys at school. But they didn't want him as a friend either. I just thought he was too weird for anybody to like, but I "had" to like him because he was my brother. It wasn't until years later that I understood why he acted that way.

It was two weeks before Christmas. I was thrilled about almost everything regarding that time of year. Those bright crayon-colored lights on our bushy tree made the dingy apartment shine like the blond hair on the doll the church had given me. My favorite spot was on the floor in front of the tree.

I'd stare at the lights while memorizing the toys on the list I'd recently mailed to Santa Claus: a shiny new Schwinn bike, roller skates, a red and white jump rope, and lots of candy. I wasn't going to give Bobby even one bite! I did ask Santa to please bring my brother a G. I. Joe toy. Of course, I was hoping all the toys would fit down the chimney. All of them! I wasn't worried because both my mother and my teacher had assured me that I had been nice, not naughty.

Now a week before Santa's visit, I looked out the front window. It had started to snow. I hated snow. It made my hands cold and I didn't like being hit by snowballs. I mean hit. The neighborhood boys would mix water in with the snow to make the snowball harder. They'd throw these ice balls at anything that moved. Bobby loved hitting me the most. There was nothing I could do except run. I couldn't tell my mother; she would have made tis come inside.

Well, on this day no one would be throwing snowballs because we had to stay in. The sidewalks and streets were so slippery that cars were spinning out of control. We hadn't been outside since moving in and Bobby was acting like the caged lion we had seen at the circus.

Searching for something to play with, lie found our mother's treasured fountain pen on the floor in her bedroom. The pen was given to her by her grandmother before she died. I didn't know what "died" meant, but I knew that playing with her pen was going to get him in trouble. I knew that if stuck with him, I'd be in trouble too.

But this was one of those rare times when my brother actually wanted me around. I felt special and honored to finally be allowed to be his friend. I didn't know then that I was developing a pattern of "doing anything to be accepted," and that proved not to be a good thing.

I laughed at Bobby as he playfully stuck our mother's fountain pen in the potbelly stove we used for heat. He was so funny and brave to get so near the flame. I rolled on the floor laughing at him. Which made him stick the pen farther into the stove. When the stove's fire caused the pen to get so hot that it burned my brother's hand, he screamed and flung the pen, which flew under the sofa. All I could think of was all my hard work at good behavior was getting ready to be wiped out. I wasn't going to ride that bike!

My parents were at work, and Mrs. Grant, the neighborhood granny and babysitter, was in the front of our shotgun-shaped apartment. (I thought she was my real grandmother because she used to rock me to sleep when I was little.) I could hear her humming what she called her "old-timey church hymn" while cooking gooey oatmeal for my sister Annette, who was three and a half, and my baby brother Larry, who was one.

And, honestly, Grandma had no idea what Bobby and I were up to. I remember thinking how glad I was that it was she who was with us now, and not our mother. My mom would have known we were up to something. My mother was the smartest woman in the world; she seemed to know exactly what we were going to do even before we did it. I now know it's because she'd "been there, done that."

I grabbed my brother and squeezed him to my chest trying to muffle his loud cries so Grandma wouldn't hear. I didn't want us to get into trouble so close to Christmas.

Bobby started wildly punching at me as if he thought I was trying to smother him. Maybe he thought I was getting even with him for calling me stupid. However, he must have finally realized by the look on my face that I was just desperately trying to keep us out of trouble, because suddenly he stopped struggling.

As he calmed down, we both got really scared when we saw his hand begin to look like he'd dipped it into red finger paint. I saw fear written on his face and knew I had to help him even though he was ruining my Christmas. I gently rubbed his hand, the way Mom did whenever we got a boo-boo. I knew he wanted Mom to do it, but my pretending to know how to make it better made the pain go away. The look in his eyes that said "thank you" was one of the reasons why I had such a strong desire to become a nurse later in life.

While I was rubbing my brother's blistered fingers, we noticed smoke coming from behind the sofa. Then we saw the beautiful flames slowly crawling up the faded white lace curtains. We were so fascinated by the red, yellow, and blue flames that we sat there staring at the fire slowly sweeping across the ceiling. I'd never seen anything so exciting. This was better than the fifteen-cent movies Mom took us to see. We could actually feel the heat and we liked it. Bobby knew that this was no movie and started looking for a way out.

Mrs. Grant had smelled the smoke and came running to our rescue. It was then I realized that being so close to flames could get you killed. Mrs. Grant grabbed us up with the speed of a bullet and shot out the door. Mrs. Grant, who before could barely make it down the stairs, suddenly became the lady in the magazine, Wilma Rudolph. She snatched my brother Larry out of his crib, put my sister Annette under her other arm, and shouted for Bobby and me to "grab a-hold of her skirt-tail." She took off like she was bringing home the gold in the Olympics.

As we ran down the stairs, she banged on the doors of the tenants housed on the other three floors, screaming "Fire!" in her out of-breath voice. When they came running out of their apartments they were forced to fall in behind Grandma, who was frantically heading for the finish line. Thank God it was early morning, because most of the people were at work. My brother and I didn't let go of Grandma's skirt-tail until we were safely outside.

I learned a valuable lesson from Grandma that day, one I wasn't even aware I was learning. It doesn't matter how old you are, you can still run a good race. For a long time after that, Mrs. Grant was my hero, and I think about her whenever I need courage.

We stood, in our PJs, in wet snow in a state of shock mingled with d read. We watched the firemen trying to put out the fire that we had so innocently started. At some point my brother and I found ourselves holding hands and from the intensity of our grasp I knew we were both thinking the same thing: Mama and Daddy are gonna kill us when they get home! We'll never be able to talk our way out of this mess!

The apartment house we called "home" burned down to the round and my parents lost everything they owned, as did everyone else. However, our parents were so happy that none of their children were hurt or killed in the fire, they grabbed us up and squeezed us like they'd never want to let go.

I was confused by their actions. I sometimes had the feeling we were in the way. The hardest thing for me had been trying to figure out how we fit into their lives. I can't explain why. I mean, I guess they loved us. They took care of us. They worked hard to buy us food and the best clothes from the second-hand store. My aunts and uncles used to tease my mother about being the only one in town with a lay-a-way plan at the Goodwill. They gave us the best their money could buy, but I felt we were supposed to also have something else. Sometimes my dad would roll on the floor and play games with us, which made me feel that at least he wanted us around.

I knew we'd done something terribly wrong by starting that fire, but somehow I was glad it happened because the fear of losing her children had caused my mother to hug my brother and me, which was something that made her uncomfortable. She usually only did that when we were at church. Most of the hugging we got came from my father. I didn't understand why my mother was that way, since the mothers of the kids at my school were always hugging their children, even when I didn't think they deserved it. It never occurred to me that maybe we weren't wanted.

It also didn't occur to me at that innocent age that they still had no idea how this fire started. When Grandma called my mother at work to tell her what had happened, she told her she had no idea what had caused it. I just knew for sure that we had been saved from "a great big ass-whooping."

The fact that we had escaped physical punishment was a miracle for us! Most black parents I knew used physical discipline back then. Coming from the Deep South, witnessing atrocities, and living in the racially biased North, Mom and Dad understood we had to "know our place in order to survive.'

But I now also believe it was a way for colored people to release their frustrations. Children were the only ones they could take it out on. They were forced to tolerate disrespect from white folks; they weren't taking it from their kids. In truth, if there had been child abuse laws in those days, both my parents would have been put underneath the jail!

My brother and I were too young to feel guilty very long about our secret. We continued in the security only a child can know and feel entitled to. That feeling began to weaken as I watched my parents sifting through the wet, stinky ashes, searching for anything left of their meager possessions.

For the first time, I sensed my parents were afraid. That night after we were all settled at Mrs. Grant's, I heard my parents whispering about their unknown future. My father had only been working for the railroad a few months and now with everything literally having gone up in smoke, he was afraid of being laid off His was one of the only jobs that offered some security to black men in those days. I realized the laughter I usually heard in my father's voice was not there.

My mom worked as a domestic for Mrs. Goldblatt, a rich white lady who paid Mom barely enough to cover living expenses for all of us. Before the fire, I'd watch my mother change leftovers into a "Sunday go-to-meeting" dinner. Now her main concern was how they would feed us. Lying on the floor at the foot of the bed, I got my first glimpse of the difference between their world and mine.

Until then I didn't realize we were in that unfortunate group known as "the poor." Poor, to me, were the children with bloated bellies that I had seen in a magazine. As I lay there listening, I imagined myself nearly naked with the distended belly, runny nose, and blank stare like in the faces of the poor children.

My parents' concerns were real but for me they still held an element of make-believe. I didn't know then, but the only money my parents had managed to save was stored safely away in the apartment along with their dreams for the future. The apartment that had burned to the ground seemed to take away their future, but somehow gave it back by the sparing of their children. I believed that money was what they were searching so hard to find in the ashes.

I'd heard one of the older ladies of the church say, "No matter how bad things gets, God always gives you what you need." I just hoped my mom and dad heard her say that too.

An unexpected act of kindness and love was shown to my parents by a few of the firemen who'd tried in vain to save our apartment building. They'd taken the time from their overworked schedule to get the necessary information to where my parents could go for assistance. I believe it was the giving atmosphere of Christmas that had caused them to open their hearts to us.

I'll never forget those sympathetic firemen who sent us to the Salvation Army for help. We ended up living in their family shelter for the next nine months, and the people who worked there were truly caring and good to us. I felt like they really wanted us there and not that we were just another poor family needing help. Lots of other families lived there too. We were the only colored one, but we weren't treated any differently by them. Everyone shared whatever they could and took turns watching each other's kids.

We had the best Christmas as children that we ever had, each of us getting all of the gifts we'd asked for. My mom and dad must have asked Santa for somewhere to live because the Salvation Army was finally able to put us in our own place. I think we were the first family to stay with them as long as we did.

They made sure to give my parents the help they needed to start over. The first three months of rent, all the furniture we needed, and a fully stocked refrigerator were paid for by donations made to the Salvation Army. I now know why those strangely dressed people who rang their bells in order to collect money for their buckets, were always standing out in the cold and snowy weather. (Today, whenever I see a donation kettle for the Salvation Army, I give gladly.)

My family settled into the new apartment at #4 Roanoke Court at the Hawkins Street housing projects to start their lives over again. It wasn't the dream house that my parents wanted to raise their family in, but they didn't have a whole lot of choice in the matter. The only thing that mattered to me was I now had plenty of space to ride my new bike, so the projects were okay with me.

However, these projects were different than the ones I had heard my mother and father talk about, the ones in the ghetto with run-down buildings and trash everywhere. Hawkins Street had plush, green, manicured lawns, and two large baseball fields surrounded by tall chain-link fences to keep the fly balls inside. Also, a huge playground and a recreation center stocked with all the neatest games. But the best part was, it stayed open seven days a week.

The living room, three bedrooms, and kitchen of our new apartment were spacious, and all were painted in an eggshell white. To us kids, we were in a new world. This was by far the nicest place we'd ever lived. I ran from room to room, spinning around in circles loving all the places I had to play in. As far as I was concerned, we had just moved into that place called Buckingham Palace. I could hardly wait to find out which of the "throne" rooms would be mine.

Bobby sat in the corner of one of the bedrooms, taking it all in but not letting me in on his thoughts. He seemed to be glued to the floor, because he didn't move at all. I guess that was his way of secretly staking his claim. My sister Annette and baby brother Larry stayed stuck right at the heels of my mom and dad, though their eyes darted all over the place. I'm sure they were confused as to why we were moving yet again. I remember my sister Annette asking Mama, ''Are we going to stay here this time?''

The families who lived in these projects were predominantly white, but they didn't seem to mind us moving in. Some of them even came by our apartment to give my parents their names and phone numbers, and to let us know we were welcome in the neighborhood. They said for us to feel free to visit them at any time. I saw little girls about my age peeping at me from behind their mothers. I could hardly wait to make new friends and get down to the business of having fun.

But school had to be taken care of before any fun and games. My brother and I were enrolled at Hawkins Street Elementary School. My classroom was huge, with lots of windows to see out of, and filled with kids. Though they looked at me strangely, they were friendly.

On my first day in the first grade I met a new friend. Her name was Gertrude. She was skinny like me, with four missing front teeth and hair the same color as my doll's. She came right up to me and started talking. She wanted _to know all about the school I came from. I wasn't able to remember the name of the school or the teacher I'd had. About the only thing I could remember was it was nothing like this one.

I'd never been to a school where I had my own new desk with a top that lifted up, where I was able to hide my books and stash of candy inside. What was really amazing to me was when I saw the gym, I couldn't believe how clean and shiny it was. Of course, I had never seen a gym before, since we didn't have one at my old school. I asked Gertrude how she got to go to such a nice school. She seemed surprised that everybody didn't.

I excitedly begged my parents to sign me up for every program the school had to offer, from violin lessons to field trips. I was so mesmerized by everything and everybody in my new environment, I soon forgot about the fire and our having to live in the projects. I didn't even feel poor anymore.

And for the first time ever, I was exposed to the world of white people. I'd heard my family talk about how white people believed they were superior to black people simply because their skin was white. They even believed that made them smarter, I'd heard.

But I could never figure out what made them think so. True enough, they had a different lifestyle. They had what appeared to be an abundance of everything compared to where I came from. There was no question they had the best books, schools, programs, and freedoms. They were free to explore, where we were taught constraint and confinement. We knew our place, so to speak.

Other than the obvious entitlements, I saw no difference. After all, we all had fingers and toes, ate food, and slept in beds. So, in my childish thinking, I led myself to believe that they were indeed different because they didn't do "number one" or "number two." White people never go to the bathroom! That had to be the difference because nothing else made any sense.

Once, when I was about nine years old, my old girlfriend Gertrude was visiting with me, and asked if she could use my bathroom. I was so curious as to what she'd do in there, I stood outside the door and listened. I got a good whiff of how wrong my thinking had been. I learned that day how incorrect thinking will cause your nose to flutter and your eyes to run water. It would take years to realize that the same incorrect thinking could and would cause pain beyond belief.

A song from the movie South Pacific describes perfectly today's status quo. The song states: "They've got to be taught before it's too late, before they are six or seven or eight, to hate all the people their relatives hate or peoples whose skin is a different hue, they've got to be carefully taught."

We learn fear and ignorance from our parents and the value system of our environment. I don't blame my parents for their incorrect understanding of people and how the world really worked. They only passed on what they were taught or had concluded from their experiences.

Chapter 2

Questionable Lane Change
"Identity Crisis"

Undoubtly, I have a very strong masculine nature that I didn't understand when I was young. All I knew was the things that most little girls, including my sister, found so fascinating, like playing with fancy dressed dolls, pretending to cook make-believe pancakes, or washing play china dishes, didn't seem to interest me at all. Over the years I tried desperately to fit in, but couldn't keep my focus on the boring "girl" games.

What my enormous curiosity craved was all the fun things that boys did. I wanted to hang out with the boys who hid behind the bushes. I could almost hear their hearts_ pounding as I waited with them to catch a ride on the freight train that ran along the tracks in the back of our projects. We'd run alongside the train as it slowed, then grab hold of the ladder and climb up on top.

At the tender age of twelve I never gave any thought to how dangerous and crazy that was. I was having fun, acting like n of the guys. We loved the thrill of running toward the front of the train trying not to fall off We'd hold our arms straight out from our sides and build up enough speed to hop from train to train. We had the best fun betting who would keep their balance. God must have been hidden in our back pockets, because nobody ever fell off.

As the train picked up speed, we'd jump off and run away as fast as we could so that the engineer couldn't see us. We'd laugh all the way home about how we'd outsmarted the engineer. I loved speed! I tried to ride my new Schwinn bike as fast as the train. I outgrew my old bike and one of my uncles surprised me with a new one for my birthday. (I didn't know it then, but he was saving his ulterior motive for lacer.)

The department store mistakenly delivered a boy's bike and offered to exchange it. I begged my uncle to let me keep it. I knew it would make all the guys jealous, and it fit the tough image I was creating. My bike was my most prized possession, my escape. I spit-shined it every day, and decorated it with red and silver plastic streamers coming out of the handlebars. This was my jet plane that took me soaring above people, buildings, and parents. I'd sometimes pretend I won a world-famous bike race and was to be the first colored person to appear on The Ed Sullivan Show to receive my well-deserved reward. I owed all the credit to the fastest bicycle in the world!

And I refused to ride a girl's bike. As a matter of fact, I started making excuses about having ugly knees and baseball bat legs in order to get out of wearing dresses after school, and I never considered putting ribbons in my hair. I tried to distance myself from anything that even suggested I was a girl. I pretended that the conversations between my girlfriends were silly. Most of the time they were. All they ever talked about was boys, and I certainly wasn't interested in making "goo-goo" eyes at no boy! I wanted to do all the fun things the guys did, but I didn't want to date them.

Besides all that, I also had a very deep voice, especially in the morning when I'd first wake up. Sometimes I'd be mistaken for a man, like when I answered the phone. It didn't bother me, though; I never desired to do "nasty things" with girls, so I knew I was okay. I didn't make the connection at the time but I now know that my acting like a tomboy had really been my remedy for keeping the_ men away.

A few months before my thirteen birthday, I found out there were a lot of men out there who used young girls as the object of their sexual fantasies. I literally had to run for my life from almost all the men who were around me. The men who were trying to molest me were the same ones I trusted to protect me. They were either trying to put their hands up my dress or crawl into bed with me while I was asleep. This included my uncles, cousins, friends of the family, and my own father.

When my dad attempted to molest me, I felt so low to the ground, dirt had to fall down on top of me. I was afraid my mother would see the dirt and ask how it got there. I wanted to tell her so that she would make it stop; but I didn't want her to know. Her lack of affection and my feelings of not being loved led me to believe that accusing her husband and brothers of something so terrible would force her to get rid of me. The conversations my mother had with her sisters, my aunts, always seemed to suggest that women deserved whatever treatment they got from men. That maybe we were even responsible for it!

I become physically ill at even the thought of telling her my father was sneaking into my room. My solution was to withdraw from both my parents. I'd hoped that would solve the problem but things only got worse. I thought the fact that my dad was among the men I had to run from was the worst thing in my life-until shortly after my fourteenth birthday.

My favorite minister sat me on his lap one Sunday after church. As we sat in the rear of the basement dining room, he began to rub his hands all over my budding breasts. My first reaction was to run. But I didn't want to hurt the feelings of my most favorite person in the universe. I remember thinking how earnestly I had prayed to God, begging him to make my dad a good man, just like the minister. All I could think now was, my dad had been doing what he was supposed to.

Then it started to feel good. My body was saying what he was doing to me had to be right, or else he wouldn't be doing it. I gave in to his touch, until I heard my soul screaming, It's wrong- that's the reason he made sure no one else was around.

Shaking off those strange new feelings, I listened to that voice, jumped off his lap, and ran like a roller coaster to tell my mother. & I burst through the door to the church I saw my mom talking with the pastor's wife. I applied the brakes to my shoes. I knew she would never believe me.

Plus, I was already in trouble. My mom had been chastising me for causing problems in my Sunday school class. I was developing a reputation among the church elders for acting "too grown." They didn't like my questioning the Sunday school teacher about the things written in the Bible. Questions like, "If Adam, Eve, Cain, and Able were the only people on earth, where did all the other people come from?"; "Is that how that thing called incest got started?" I wanted to know why the baby doll used for the role of Jesus had blond hair and blue eyes. I thought that was a reasonable question since I was playing the role of his mother, Mary.

My questions caused the seniors to be upset with me. They said I was sassy and should never question God. I told them I wasn't questioning God, I was asking them. They acted as if my words were equal to punching God in the eye. The "color" actually drained from their faces, and they refused to talk any further with me.

My parents treated me as if my thirst for knowledge had caused them to get a bad mark on their Christian report card. I wasn't trying to cause trouble; I just needed to make sense of the stories told in Sunday school. But the elders took my inquiries as a lack of respect for them and the Church.

I knew if I said anything about what had taken place in the basement, they'd have me tarred and feathered. They wouldn't hesitate to say that I had caused the good pastor to go astray. I decided it would be best to keep my lips glued together. I was trapped in a world of silence.

And I hated the pastor for forcing me there and for his taking away the love I'd developed for him. His actions affected me more than the common man because I had him "right up therewith God." I really believed he could walk on water. I expected to see the parting of the Red Sea whenever he raised his hands for the congregation to stand. Those same hands that held the Holy Bible now wanted to a caress my body. Not only did he hurt my soul, he helped give me the low opinion I had of myself, and a false understanding of right and wrong. Was I wrong to reject the advances of men? Was the pastor right ? Should I tell God on him?

Later on when I heard him preach about Jezebel, an evil woman who seduced men, I assumed he was directing his sermon at me. I felt deeply ashamed, and was naive enough to believe that I had somehow been responsible for his unwanted behavior. I felt guilty. Guilty for not telling and guilty for responding to his touch. Why did it feel so good if it was wrong? Why did he choose me?

I questioned myself: Had I been giving off "sensual" signals without knowing it, causing this dedicated man of God to be drawn to me? Maybe I deserved what was happening to me. I wish I could've told my mother what was going on with me, but I never felt close enough to her to share my feelings.

I remember once being in church sitting next to my mother. I inched over until I was close enough to lay my head on her shoulder. I was hoping she'd put her arms around me and pull 'me close. Instead, I felt her body stiffen as if she'd been frightened by something horrible. She quickly dropped her shoulder down, causing my head to fall off I felt demons must be inside me. Why else would she pull away?

I knew my mother would never find out what was going on.

Her attitude toward me was that I always caused her problems.

I couldn't imagine her talking with me about anything. She was probably afraid to ask questions she really didn't want answers to. She'd never ask why I no longer wanted to visit with the pastor and his wife, or why the mention of his name caused me to shake and put a frown on my face. She acted as if she hadn't noticed how quiet I'd gotten.

However, I had no idea she thought my behavior was strange or abnormal, until the day she said, 'I'm concerned that you haven't started your monthly."

I was fifteen, and most of my girlfriends had already started their menstrual cycle before that age. My mother told me that she was going to take me to the doctor to find out why I hadn't started yet. Of course, I didn't care if it ever got started. To me, that was just another one of those "girl things" that I could definitely live without.

Weeks later, after Dr. Pansa examined me, I stood outside his office door and overheard the real reason my mother had made the appointment. She asked him if he thought I might be gay, because I never showed any curiosity in doing the things that other girls my age did. It seemed strange to her that I didn't show any interest in dating or liking boys at all. Not that she really wanted me to, since I was barely fifteen; but it seemed the natural thing for young girls to do.

Hearing my mother ask the doctor that question made me feel that maybe something was wrong with the way that I was reacting to the world. Here I was thinking the reason my mom didn't like me was because I always caused problems.

This new revelation made my brain do backward flips! Why would my mother ask the doctor a question like that? Why wouldn't she talk to me about it? How could she think that about her own daughter? I never thought of myself as being gay. I liked girls; I even thought some of them were pretty, but I didn't want to be in love with them or have sex with them. Maybe if I could tell her about my father, she'd understand. But then again, if my own mother thought that I was gay, maybe I was and I just didn't know it. Life was beginning to feel like a scary Halloween night.

Today, whenever I'm invited to speak to young girls who find themselves in a situation like mine, or worse, I always tell them: Never let fear stop you from removing yourself from a situation if it does not feel right in your soul. And to always tell some-

body you trust, what's going on. Not telling what was happening in my life inadvertently led to my having even more bad experiences.

Chapter 3

Shining Headlights Straight Ahead
"Challenging Family Values"

I was, deep down, determined to find out if I was gay or not, and I knew how I was going to do it. A guy named Johnny, who hung out with our group, confided to a mutual friend-who immediately told me-that he thought I was cute. I thought Johnny was cute, too, and he had the coolest walk I'd ever seen. He'd cock his head to the side, lean his body to the right with the right arm remaining stiff as the left swung back and forth to the rhythm in each dip of his step.

I already knew I liked him because I became nervous and shy whenever he was around, even though I never_ thought about going to any of the neighborhood dances with him. I wasn't interested in boys to that degree. I was also afraid they'd find out what the grownup men had been doing to me, and wouldn't want me.

But I was now on a mission of self-discovery. I decided it was time for me to stash my Schwinn, put on a prissy dress, weave some colored ribbons into my hair, and get to know cool-walking Johnny even better.

I made it known through our mutual friend that I'd like Johnny to ask me to the weekly neighborhood party. Before the end of the week he managed to get up enough nerve to ask me to the party and get my parents' consent. My mother flashed the biggest smile of relief, and only I knew what was behind it. I felt she was happy at the thought of not having a troublesome and weird daughter.

Both mentally and physically, I spent the entire week getting ready for my big night out. I borrowed an armload of love novels from my girlfriends and read them cover to cover, gathering valuable information on what to do on a first date. I decided to wear my red and white polka-dot dress with the white lace collar, the one that made me look older. I ironed it over and over to make sure it was perfect. The look of approval on Johnny's face when he came to pick me up let me know my efforts had not been in vain.

I sat on his lap at the Saturday night party, pretending to

know how this "boy and girl thing" went. I hoped I wouldn't have flashbacks of my abuse; it would cause me to feel too dirty to continue. When he put his arms around me and drew me dose to him, I tried to relax and act the way I saw Lana Turner do in the movies, and the way the love novels described it. I was pulling off my act just fine, until he stuck his tongue down my throat! I jumped two feet in the air and wiped my mouth with the back of my hand. Nothing I had ever seen or read prepared me for that. I never saw Lana Turner with a tongue down her throat. I thought the leading men who kissed her did so with their mouths dosed. After all, they slept in twin beds and wore pajamas.

Johnny was a few years older than I, and no doubt had this romance business down to a science. It didn't take him long to figure out I didn't know anything about what really went on between a man and a woman. My experience so far had only caused repulsion and shame. He took me by my hand and began to patiently explain,

"I wasn't doing anything bad. This is the way two people kiss when they really like each other." He said all the things I needed to hear to have the courage to complete my mission. He made me feel special. No one had ever held me close or talked so sweetly to me before. I reluctantly sat back down on his lap.

We kissed again; but this time he slowly moved a hand over my breasts. My skin began to get hot, and I knew the fire roaring inside my body was going to burn me up if it wasn't put out soon.

I was so ravaged by these new sensations, I agreed to leave the party and go up the street with him to his friend Ted's apartment. I knew what Johnny had on his mind. And my mind was thinking, After tonight, I'll know for sure if I should continue wearing a dress or learn how to use a hammer.

Although I wasn't aware of it at the time, Ted's bachelor apartment was designed for the sole purpose of seduction. The radio was tuned to WDAS, the only black station in Newark. Saturday night was when they played popular love songs. Tonight they played all my favorites. This of course helped to set the mood.

The light bulbs were blue, making the apartment so dark it took a few minutes for my eyes to adjust. The walls throughout most of Ted's apartment were painted a passionate red. The cocoa brown carpet in the living room and bedroom was as soft as a feathered pillow. The bedroom was exceptionally dark because of the heavy green curtains covering the window. The only furniture in the entire room was a huge four-poster bed, with four massive purple pillows on a green and white bedspread.

Johnny began to undress as soon as he guided me into the bedroom. I stood there trembling, wondering if I really needed to know the truth about my gender. I couldn't imagine taking all my clothes off in front of any man. He sensed that I was trying to back out of the scene, so he put his arms around me, drew me to him, kissed me long and passionately, then gently pulled me down on the bed and turned off the light. My lights went on!

Forget all the bullshit you just read about my "seduction," because that was my made-up Hollywood version. We actually went down to the basement and did our thing on the cement floor, with my freshly ironed, polka-dotted dress up around my neck. Okay, so how many teenagers have an apartment to go to and do their thing? Do you know any?

Though I enjoyed the kissing and touching, I felt nothing but pain when it came to the actual act of lovemaking. I wondered, Is this how Adam and Eve started creation? Had it been Eve's idea to procreate, or was it Adam's brainstorm?

I was still as confused about my sexual identity as ever. I thought it was going to be like in the movies, with fireworks exploding and violins playing beautiful music. Like most people, I'd been programmed by Hollywood to believe that was how things actually happened. I was now being shown the movie called "Reality"!

As soon as the actual act of lovemaking began, all of Johnny's comforting words disappeared. What seemed to matter to him was experiencing whatever it was that caused his eyes to roll back in his head and his body to quiver, as he screamed out loud "Oh shit baby!" He never once heard my cries.

Walking home that night, we didn't hold hands or look into each other's eyes with undying love because I was too embarrassed to look at him. This is not what I had expected sex to be. The ripping, cutting feeling between my legs made me ask myself if I even liked him. Do men hurt like this? I was trying to be cool, but I felt like I had done something terribly wrong. And then the thought struck Johnny was in another world; he seemed to be floating. His chest stuck way out and he had the smile of "being first" stretched across his face. My girlfriend Gertrude once told me that when a man treads where no one else has before, it "puts a notch in his belt." I looked down at Johnny's belt, but wasn't able to see anything in the dark.

I wondered how my mother had felt the first time she made love. But it was difficult for me to imagine my mother doing such a thing in the first place. If I weren't sitting here alive today, I would doubt she had ever done such a thing as have sex with my father. And I certainly couldn't imagine my wanting to ever do such a painful, humiliating thing again Did that mean that I was gay?

I blamed everyone and everything, from my parents to Hollywood movies, for my lack of good judgment. But back then, there was no information about being gay, or the difference between sex and love. Parents didn't know to educate their children about safe sexual practices or to establish a relationship where children felt safe to talk to them about their emotions.

Johnny told me he was in love and he wanted us to have a permanent relationship. I was struggling within myself, trying to find a way to tell him I wasn't sure if I wanted anything to do with love, since, really, I'd only been on "a mission."

Ironically, however, Uncle Sam saved me from having to explain myself and thereby helped me avoid having to deal with what would've been a bad situation. When Johnny called, I could tell from the sound of his shaky voice that he had tears in his eyes: "I just got a letter from the government, Rose. I've been drafted."

His news made me both happy and sad at the same time. I was happy because now I didn't have to break his heart by telling him he'd been my guinea pig. I was sad because I remembered hearing my father say, "Most colored men who go to war, come back home in a body bag."

I liked Johnny and I wanted to be his friend. I wanted him to stay alive so he could be happy and find that perfect mate I knew he deserved. Someone who didn't have dark secrets. I wasn't sure if I would ever have any real feelings of love for any man. How could I ever trust them?

Johnny had been gone only a few months when I had my sixteenth birthday, and started waking up in the morning feeling nauseated.

Of course, being the knowledgeable person about life that I was, putting the facts of morning sickness together with being pregnant was not in my range of understanding. I was thinking that maybe I should ask my mother to give me some medicine because I must have caught the flu. I had no idea my situation was going to skyrocket my mind to a whole different level. I didn't understand how I could get pregnant without being in love or married. I was still living in Hollywood!

***

I was babysitting for my mom's brother, Uncle Isaiah, when he saw me put my hand over my mouth and make a mad dash for the bathroom. He said, "The only time I've seen a woman do that, she was pregnant. Is that your problem?"

The question hit me like that tree I ran into while riding my bike. Another wave of nausea erupted in my stomach as if to confirm his suspicions. I didn't know how to answer him. I knew deep down inside he was right and that had to be what was wrong with me. But my soul was saying, This can't be happening to me, and I'm not ready to be a mother. I don't even know how!

I stared at my uncle, wishing a black hole would open up and swallow me. That would have been a better fate for me than facing my parents.

My uncle took me home, gathered my mama and daddy together, and seated them on the living room sofa. As he delivered the 'unwelcome news, they sat there in silence, stunned and staring straight ahead. It was as if my uncle was the coroner telling them their daughter died. My mother looked as if she wished I were already in the ground.

I pressed myself deeper into the love seat, trying to disappear. Their eyes slowly shifted to me. No words were said, but I could hear the questions screaming out at me: "What have we done wrong?" "Why did it ...?" "When did it ...?" "Where did it ...?"

After a few minutes, though, they were able to somehow get past their shock and demanded to know who the father was.

Hawkins Street projects had changed over the years. Whenever a black family moved in, three white families moved out. I knew my parents were mentally going through all the new faces of the young men who had recently come to our house.

I opened my mouth but shame had robbed me of my ability to speak. I managed to make my lips work and, finally, in a voice barely above a whisper, I told them, "It was Johnny. Johnny did it all."

I had to blame Johnny. After all, he was older. He "knew better." But I was guilty too. I had planned the whole scene. I watched my mother slump down into the sofa and drop her head. I knew she was thinking about how happy she'd been when I finally put on a dress and went to the party, and how relieved she felt seeing I was actually a straight woman after all. But she hadn't counted on my becoming that much of a woman so soon.

I wondered what my father was thinking. He had stopped trying to put his hands up my dress when I started wearing pants. He was probably afraid I'd tell. I was thinking he had no right to judge me and should actually be willing to help.

* * *

I kept trying to make sense of the situation. I wondered, How could I be pregnant? I've only started to menstruate within the last few months and I had only one period before my night of lovemaking with Johnny. Sure, I was aware I hadn't menstruated for the past two months, but I thought the reason for that was because I was going through that "change of life" thing I'd heard my mother talk about with some of the women from the church. They said you no longer had a period when you were going through "the change." That had to be what was wrong with me. I had only had sex one time; certainly it took more than that! I know now, but that was the day I broke my own record for being deep but shallow.

***

I reluctantly wrote to Johnny and told him of the predicament we were in. He wrote me back, saying, "'As soon as I come home on leave, I want to do the honorable thing and marry you." I was hoping he'd say he would bring money for my abortion. I'd never wanted to play house, and I certainly didn't want to be married.

I told Johnny I wasn't ready to be anybody's wife. I knew he hadn't given serious thought to the fact that his hangout time would be over. He'd now have the huge responsibility of a wife and baby. If he had, I'm sure he would have realized, like I had, that he wasn't really in love with me. He was just living out the same Hollywood movie script as I was: We would get married, have children, get a house with a white picket fence, and live happily ever after.

The concept of being a mother and marrying someone I didn't love, though, caused me to spend hours staring at the blank walls in my room. I was searching both for a way out and to avoid seeing my mom's and dad's disappointment in me.

I was surprised and relieved when my parents didn't force me to get married. I believe they based that decision on their own lives.

I couldn't know for sure, but I believed my father loved my mother yet couldn't make her happy. She resented getting pregnant and didn't really love my father. She probably sensed his hidden traits of indiscretion and knew she could never trust him. My mother had a free spirit and would have explored everything the world had to offer if she wouldn't have had the obligation of raising a family. I think she would have been the "colored" version of Amelia Earhart! But in her time, if a woman found herself pregnant, she had no choice but to marry; and you were considered a social outcast if you didn't. There was no such thing as a single mother, unless you were a widow.

I didn't know it at the time, but that was the reason my parents had to marry. Knowing that about my mother now helps me understand the kind of woman she was. She had to accept the responsibility of her "mistake" even though it meant the death of her dreams. I don't think my father ever understood that about her.

After the first few years of living in the projects, my father developed a problem with alcohol. He didn't drink constantly, but regularly drank his red liquor on weekends. However, he made sure he was sober for church on Sunday. That was the good part. The bad part was, as he drank he spent all of the money we needed to live on, which ultimately made the situation worsen between my parents.

It seemed all it took to start a heated argument between them was for one of them to say good morning in the "wrong" tone of voice. I don't recall ever seeing my mother and father in a loving embrace. I began to believe he drank because he didn't feel worthy of my mother and because of our hidden secret. Reflecting on their experience helped me understand why they didn't want me to go through that kind of bondage.

It was remarkable to me that, just as my parents were doing their best to deal with my situation and trying to stand up straight, the steamroller of bad news once again flattened them to the ground.

I found out that my younger sister Annette-who everyone thought was an angel-was also pregnant. At fourteen, my sister had grown into a woman without my ever noticing. Even though we shared the same bedroom, we didn't tell each other our secrets.

I think she thought I was too rebellious to be relating with her like a real sister. I was busy breaking all the rules while she was obeying every one of them. Or so I thought. Actually, I didn't even know that "Miss Goody Two Shoes" had a boyfriend.

When she heard about my predicament, she felt confident enough to reveal her secret to me. I was so surprised by her revelation that I didn't think to ask her who the father was. She was hoping I'd be the one to break the news to my parents, but I couldn't imagine being the bearer of that news.

I was trying to stay out of Mom and Dad's way because they were still struggling to accept what was happening with me. I imagined a funeral hearse driving slowly through the projects and coming to a full stop in front of our apartment. They would be there to pick up the bodies of my sister and me, because I knew there was no way we were coming out of this alive!

Unbeknown to us, our brother Bobby was listening outside our bedroom door and overheard Annette telling me her secret. He could hardly wait to tell my parents, and even though I tried, it was too late to catch him. He could've won an Olympic gold medal for his record-breaking delivery of the heart-shattering news.

As my selfish brother stood against the wall gloating, I watched the color drain from my mother's face, to end up faded as the many loads of laundry she'd washed all those years. My father sat there in silence, his face wedged between his hands. As parents, they felt they were failures. No one in our neighborhood had ever had two teen-aged daughters pregnant at the same time. How could they go anywhere in the community, even to church, without feeling guilty? This wasn't a secret that could be hidden.

My mother's hand was shaking as she pointed her finger in the direction of our room and demanded that we go there. They were too distressed to ask my sister who was responsible for her being in the family way. At that point they were probably too broken down to care. They were so desperate to find a solution to their undeserved nightmare, they took a big helping of bad advice from some of our relatives.

Soon after the word got out, Uncle Isaiah told my parents they should put us in a home for unwed mothers. It was a logical way to solve their unwanted problem because the home would put the babies up for adoption as soon as they were born. When my parents agreed with him, he made all the arrangements for our stay. Apparently, it sounded like a good idea to my parents; no one would see us walking around the neighborhood pregnant, and their "reputation" would be preserved from further tarnish. My sister and I were told that we were scheduled to leave for the home within two weeks; and we had no say in the matter. Back then the rule was: Children should be seen but not heard.

I don't recall the name of the small town in New Jersey where the home was located, nor do I remember much about the people who lived or worked there-except they were all white. I didn't know any colored girls who were sent away to have their babies. They had the baby at home, and the family raised it. I guess their parents loved them too much to be ashamed. My parents sat stiffly at the desk of the head nurse and cemented the arrangements for our stay at the St. James Home for unwed mothers.

My sister and I were assigned to a small, white bedroom located on the first floor. We each had our own closet, and there were twin beds with matching bedspreads adorned with prints of colorful butterflies. With the exception of the beautiful bedspreads, the twin beds reminded me of home. That revelation did nothing to calm my fears as we said goodbye to my parents.

My sister and I decided since we were the ones who were "different," we'd better stay dose together. The stern-looking, blond haired head nurse gruffly explained that the house rules would allow us to go home on weekends, with the consent of our parents.

Annette was still angry that my parents had sent us here, so she said, "They can keep their guilty weekend visits. Whenever I leave this place, I'll be moving straight into my own apartment t." This was the first time my sister had shared anything with me. Her strong will eased my fears. She was determined to do it all on her own, even down to keeping her baby's father a secret. I smiled at my little sister and admired the calm control she seemed to have. I thought, She should have been the older sister.

I wrote to Johnny every day, filling him in on the events since he was the only one I could talk to about what was happening. He told me he'd be coming home soon and would take me back with him as his wife. He assumed that his plan would be better for me than the alternative. I felt that I was treading water in the middle of a stormy sea, with a man I didn't love trying to save me from the hungry sharks.

Before we left for the home, my mother's sister, Aunt Marie, gave her some small, black, gel-like pills and told her if she were to give us two pills each, it would cause us to miscarry. From a medium, Aunt Marie had gotten information of someone who specialized in getting rid of unwanted babies. My desperate mother, without telling my father, gave those pills to both of us.

I didn't ask my mother what the pills were for. I mistakenly assumed that she had accepted the situation and was merely giving us pills the doctor had prescribed. I gladly took my two pills because I'd have done anything if it would make my mother not be mad at me anymore.

My sister put the pills under her tongue and pretended to swallow them. She must have overheard my aunt when she told my mother what they were for. I didn't want to know anything, so I didn't ask her if she knew what the pills what the pills were for. My sister had secretly vowed to keep her baby and was suspicious of any act of kindness from my mother. She said she had to keep her baby so that she'd have someone who could truly love her'.

I didn't write and tell Johnny about the pills; I sensed that this was something he wouldn't like.

A few months went by without anything happening. Then, one weekend, while I was home for a rare visit, I started to have cramps in my stomach. They were so severe that I felt like my intestines were going to burst. I briefly thought it might be that I needed to have a bowel movement. I wanted to ask my mother if this was how things were supposed to be, but hearing anything about my plight always made her angry with me all over again. When the pain got worse, I got up from my bed and went to the bathroom. As I sat on the toilet, I noticed some blood spots on the bathroom floor. The sight of that blood put a big smile on my face.

I thought, Great, my period is back! I'm not pregnant. I wanted so badly for things to be like they were before. I actually believed the baby growing inside of me would disappear and everything would be normal again. Only someone as foolish as I could have had such ridiculous thoughts.

My happiness turned to terror when I felt something moving between my legs. I looked down and saw a small foot moving around, as if trying to get back inside. I screamed for my mama. She ran to the bathroom and found me on the floor, along with more blood.

I was expecting my mother-who could never stand the sight of blood-to start screaming as loud as I was. Instead, I heard her say, as she ran to call the ambulance, "I thought this day was never gonna happen! This is what I've been waiting for." I wondered, What does she mean by that? I wouldn't know the answer to that question for years, but at that moment I knew it was somehow connected to those pills.

The doctors rushed to work on me as soon as I was brought into the emergency room. I felt terrified and totally alone. I didn't know if my mother was at the hospital or not because she hadn't ridden in the ambulance. The prognosis was critical, since toxic poison had flooded my system as a result of the pills my mother had given me. The doctors gave me something to induce labor, in order to try and save the life of the baby. I felt as if my entire body was being ripped in half. I begged for medicine for my pain, but was only given cold hard stares by the nurses.

It wasn't known until I was eighteen hours into my labor that my birth canal was too small to have a normal delivery. And the baby was coming out feet first, complicating matters even further.

I was hoping like I'd never hoped before that my mother was somewhere nearby and would hear my screams. I wanted her to wrap her arms around me and take me back to the time before I went on my "mission."

But, if she heard me, she didn't come. I felt abandoned by my parents and betrayed by Donna Stone and June Cleaver. They had made it look all so simple, holding their newborns and displaying a pain-free smile to the audience. Here I was getting yet another lesson about the "Hollywood illusion" of life.

The doctors tried everything to turn the baby but nothing worked; and it was too late for a cesarean section. The only alternative was to use forceps to get the baby out, because the unusual positioning of the body made any other delivery impossible. After what seemed like the changing of all the seasons, the worst experience of my life was finally over. In the end, the doctors managed to save only my life. My son died from a broken neck. I couldn't bring myself to name the baby boy who had come from inside of me.

Just when I thought the pain was over, I was subjected to the cruel, biased beliefs of the hospital staff, attitudes like: "You shouldn't be pregnant in the first place"; '_'You're colored and too poor to have a baby!", etc. I felt no compassion or mercy from them; instead I felt judged and left to deal with my own pain, which was truly devastating.

I awoke in the hospital ward the next morning to the sight of my mother sitting in the chair next to my bed. She was staring at the floor. I studied her and realized she was always distant; I don't remember her ever hugging or kissing us, or telling us that she loved us.

Up until that moment I believed that every woman who experienced birth automatically loved her children. I longed to tell my mother that I now understood how a woman is sometimes forced by unforeseen circumstances to play a role that she didn't audition for. I could now relate to why it had been difficult for her to embrace me. I ached for my mother to put her arms around me and tell me that everything was going to be all right.

Instead, she acted as if my pregnancy was the worst thing that could have ever happened to her. Every time I reached out to my mother, hoping to touch her heart, her frozen attitude toward me led me to believe that our relationship would always remain in the iceberg stage.

A vision of my friend, Gertrude, popped into my mind. I envied the relationship she shared with her mother. They could talk about anything, and Gertrude knew she was loved, no matter what mistakes she made. I knew that if my sister had been there I could count on her for comfort. We had become almost like best friends over the last few months. I hoped she'd be allowed to visit me, because I wanted to warn her of the humiliating experience she'd have to endure. And simply for not having the blessing of some man's last name.

I stared at the new mothers feeding their babies, and I wondered what it was like to have such joy about giving birth. All I felt was relief I hadn't wanted baby, and the fact that he hadn't survived seemed like the answer to my prayers. Harboring such horrible thoughts made me feel like the lowest, dirtiest thing on the planet, like a cold hearted monster.

I interpreted my mother's resentment and lack of affection or support for me as something wrong with me. Maybe she saw herself in me and it reminded her of her past. I was afraid that since I was a part of her, I would inherit her inability to love, so I vowed never to have children. I truly believed I would have made a lousy mother.

I tried everything I could to make my mother forget this horrible "incident" and forgive me for disappointing her. I ended my relationship with Johnny, and swore off ever dating again. I tried to do every chore my mother assigned. I came home before curfew. Still, nothing worked. My mother never trusted or believed in me again. My sister accepted the fact that our mother's shame about the errors in her life would never allow her to accept our "shortsightedness." But I refused to believe her heart could be so unforgiving. Sadly, things only got worse between us.

I spent years blaming my mother for all of my bad experiences. I convinced myself that it was her fault I'd gotten pregnant. After all, if she had loved me more, I wouldn't have slept with the first man who said he liked me. That selfish reasoning caused me a lot of unnecessary grief. My parents both did the best they could for their family, even though they weren't financially or emotionally prepared for one. It was easier to blame the, lack of hugs and kisses than it was for me to create the life I wanted. It doesn't matter who your parents are, or how many setbacks you experience; you and only you can give your soul joy. I took a lot of whippings (not physical, but psychological and emotional ones) before I finally learned that lesson.

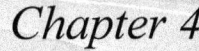

Chapter 4

Moving in Reverse
"Like a Donkey Carrying Books"

***T**here* were laws against being a pregnant student in 1959. New Jersey law held that if a student became pregnant, she was not allowed to return to school. Since my parents wanted me to finish high school, they agreed that I should stay with my grandmother, who lived in Philadelphia, so that I could continue my education. I felt their decision to "ship me out" had nothing to do with my receiving a diploma.

I believed that they wanted me out of town before anyone would see me. No one except my immediate family and Johnny knew that my sister and I were pregnant, and I had sworn him to secrecy. Everyone else had been informed that Annette and I were enrolled in a "better" school out of state. My mom and dad feared the curious questions my friends would ask as to why I'd come back home. That old New Jersey law had only been a ploy:

At that time I hadn't been allowed to talk to my sister, so I had no way of knowing if she had been told about my giving birth, .or of my being exiled to Philadelphia.

I sat on the gold silk pillow inside my grandmother's bay window, and watched my parents' car drive away.

My version of a made-up movie started to play in my mind: The car stops, my parents burst out of the door and run to me with outstretched arms. They held me tightly to their chest and begin passionately hugging and kissing me, and begging my forgiveness for having left me at my grandmother's.

The reality was, they didn't even look back. I made up my mind that day that no one would ever love me, and I might as well continue to self destruct.

When my grandmother would take her regular afternoon nap, I'd sneak a phone call to my sister. Annette was still living at the home and was within two weeks of delivery. She'd tell me how scared she was and I'd reassure her the best I knew how. After I told her of Mom's cold reaction to my pain and suffering during the delivery, Annette was more determined than ever not to go back home. Our shared moments of anguish back then caused us to become as dose as twins.

Even so, she still refused to share with me the name of her baby's father. Whenever I'd ask her, she'd say, "I'm the mother and the father." Because of her strong refusal to name her baby's father, I briefly wondered if any of the men in my family, who'd chased me throughout my puberty, had caught my sister. She told me about some of her other secrets. Like having her own apartment and raising her baby by herself, was shame the reason she wouldn't share the father's name with me?

I knew my parents weren't aware that my sister had no intention of giving her baby away. She said the information would be more than my mother could bear and it would break her heart. Like me, I knew deep down she still loved my mother and didn't want to hurt her. We talked about the possibility of our getting an apartment together; but we knew at least for now, it was just a dream. All we knew how to do was go to school, go to church, and visit our aunts and uncles.

Staying with my grandmother was totally different than living with my parents. She was older and not quite as attentive to what I was up to as my parents had been. I found, for the first time in my life, that I had freedom, and that freedom without responsibility was' a dangerous thing.

I attended William Penn High School, a girl's school which was located across the street from Benjamin Franklin High, a boy's school. For the first time since kindergarten I was in a school with only colored kids.

There was a little Italian sandwich shop, Tony Meat Balls, down the street, which was a gathering place for kids from both schools.

When I could no longer stomach the bland school lunch, I'd head straight to Tony's for a delicious bologna and cheese sandwich on a hard roll, dripping with mayonnaise---exactly what a teenager with no concept of a balanced diet would crave. The sandwiches and sodas filled my stomach so full I thought it, would explode.

However, the hunger for their food didn't compare with the excitement I felt from being around most of the kids who hung out there. A lot of the teenagers at Tony's seemed to have it "going' on." The girls wore the latest style poodle skirts with a ton of crinoline slips. They gave an extra spin as they entered the door, to make the skirt flair. The black and white saddle oxfords were glistening dean. The guys all walked cool, talked cool, and played it cool by ruffing up the sleeves on their white T-shirts.

It seemed the food was only an excuse for being there. Everyone really showed up to be chosen or accepted by one group or another. It was there that I met my future partner in crime, Earl "Gufy Cook." They called him Gufy because his right foot looked goofy when he walked. He had tried to sneak a ride on the side of a trolley one day and the wheels literally amputated his toes. When he walked, he'd leaned over to his right side, bend down low and stroll, adding a little dip to his stride so no one would notice he had a limp. He reminded me of Johnny, except he wasn't as handsome. Gufy hung out with a group of guys that seemed to always be doing interesting, forbidden things: shoplifting, smoking pot, and the like. The only people I'd seen do anything like that had been on the big screen; so naturally, I wanted to fit in with these "happening" guys.

Gufy and I started hanging together; and because I was cool, like a guy, before long the others began to accept me as part of the gang. I liked Gufy because he respected and protected me. Though he never hit on me and he always treated me like a friend, Gufy made it dear to the rest of the gang that "Nobody bet' not mess with huh." Gufy was street tough and all the guys were afraid of him.

At twenty-one years old, Big Marvin was the oldest of the group. Some of the guys referred to him as Fat Marvin because he was as round as all the jelly donuts he had eaten. He was also the only one with a job and his own apartment, which we all used as "our hangout crib." Like most men, he wasn't big on the art of decorating. His one-bedroom apartment consisted of a wrought-iron bed, a "dirty blue" love seat sofa, and a wooden kitchen table with two wobbly chairs. We all thought it was cool.

Billy was the gang member who the rest of us felt had the brains; maybe it was because he was the one who'd finished high school. Anyway, since his hair was wavy and he bore a slight resemblance to Frederick Douglass, Billy often thought of himself as a modern-day version of the great nineteenth-century abolitionist. Whenever someone made the unfortunate mistake of asking him a question on the topic of the day, they got a dose of his warped opinion about life.

I discovered he wasn't a total egomaniac, however, when he offred to teach me how to drive. His patience and calming presence led me to believe that there was a real gentleman hiding inside him, just waiting to be born.

We had a few other gang members, all of whom had their own special character. Wallace was known by the people in the neighborhood as a poet. He wrote a poem for every girl he was dating, and they all believed the words were written just for them. Slim was the tall, light-skinned, pimply-faced silent one. All he ever did was flash his dopey-looking smile and do whatever we told him to. Even his four-foot-tall girlfriend bossed him around.

James was the most handsome man of the group and he knew it. He was the only one with a mustache, and he washed his three changes of clothes every night. The crease in his pants was as sharp as a razor and he was always sporting' a fresh haircut. He could never walk past a mirror without spending a few minutes in awe of himself Milton reminded me of a colored version of Humphrey Bogart. He had a frown on his face and always wanted to beat up somebody. He only stood five feet, seven inches tall, but he was tougher than Jack Johnson, the prize fighter.

Everyone in our gang was fascinated by the gangster movies of the day, especially the ones featuring Edward G. Robinson, James Cagney, and Bogie. We wanted to be like them, walk like them, talk like them, dress like them, and do the scary, thrilling things they did-especially things that were outside of the law.

During this time in my life I learned some valuable lessons on how men think. Lessons that would help and guide me all through my life. Most men don't have a lot of respect for what women are able to do. I wanted to be as good, if not better, at everything they did. If they were target-shooting and struck the chest, I wanted to hit dead center in the head.

The only thing I was not interested in competing with was the sexual exploitation by the guys. I simply observed and kept my mouth shut. My silence made them lower their guard even more and openly discuss women the way only men can. They seemed to find excitement in the hunt and capture of a woman. Once that's achieved they became bored and ready to move on to the next victim. Not all of the guys felt that way, but what an education I got. It only helped confirm my feelings that men are only good to hang out with.

I started lying to my grandmother about my whereabouts. My parents' phone calls to check on my activities became sporadic, enabling me to disappear for longer and longer periods of time.

A few months into the twelfth grade, I decided I'd had enough of school. I quit without telling my parents and began hanging out with the guys more and more. After all, I was almost eighteen. I felt as if getting on with growing up was important, and hanging with the guys played a large part in that process.

Don't Blame The Road

We'd stand around outside Morgan's Bar on the corner of Eighth and Columbia Avenues, checking out everything and everybody in the neighborhood. Dixon's Hoagie Shop was right across the street supplying the food we would chip in to buy. Big Marvin was the only one old enough to go inside the bar, so he would buy beer for all the younger guys. I didn't need the beer; I got drunk on the happenings.

There would always be loud music blaring out of the barroom door, and the ladies inside would be shaking their "big booties" to the beat of The Temptations. Every so often, one of the crazy neighborhood dudes got a little too drunk and would start a fight, simply because he thought somebody had said something derogatory about his "old lady." During one of those fights, somebody yelled "He's got a gun," and those Negroes come scrambling out of the door as if he'd screamed "Bomb!"

Such events made it all the more exciting to hang around in our gang. I felt as if I was a member of a family that had all kinds of people in it.

I don't think any of us planned on becoming criminals; it just seemed to go with our attitude of being tough. None of us ever considered hurting anyone, or ever pondered the fact that, while doing what we were doing, any one of us could get shot or killed.

Our first theft was not even planned; it sort of happened. One evening we were walking home from Morgan's Bar and one of the guys spotted these shiny chrome hubcaps on an old, beat-up car. We thought it was stupid to put something so pretty on something so ugly, and Gufy said, "Let's steal them." It was so much fun that as we ran off, someone said, "Hey, let's steal a car, too!"

We targeted Chevy Impalas, since they were easy to start if the ignition wasn't turned off properly. We would travel across the Benjamin Franklin Bridge to Camden, New Jersey, to steal cars because it would take the police longer to find them. That way we could joyride to Atco, New Jersey, for a whole week before having to ditch them. Atco was a mini Atlantic City minus the slot machines. A postage-stamp-sized beach was dotted with juke joints and barbecue shacks. We easily found the many dirt roads. One in particular was used by the locals as a racetrack, and we quickly made u e of it.

We frequented a place there called Shuggs. One night after drag racing we headed home only to find we did not have the toll. Since I was driving and I knew no fear, I decided to run the toll booth. The chase was on. The bridge police chased me into Philly. I shot down a one-way street that they missed. That gave us a chance to park the car, get out and sit on someone's steps, and watch the police come up the street. When they stopped, we told them "We saw them jump out and run that way."

I look back now and I am afraid. Then, I was too young and wild. I was seeking acceptance and didn't know that at any turn my life could have been forfeited. That is the mentality of gangs today.

One day, James got hold of a gun and we decided to see if we could pull off a robbery, like we had seen in the movies. We decided to hold up the service station located on Jefferson Street, not far from Morgan's. The station was a lopsided, rusted-out building, with dirty restrooms and gum on the floors. We felt that since it was close to where we hung out, it would be easy for us to make our escape.

Just as it got dark that Friday night, I drove the stolen getaway car to the station. I was chosen to be the driver because I was a girl, and because I was also crazy enough to take a curb at a hundred miles an hour. Billy sat next to me while Slim, James, Wallace, and Gufy sat in the back seat. We didn't do a lot of talking on the way there. It was understood that I'd remain in the car while the guys went in to do the job.

As soon as they opened the car door to get out, my knees started shaking. I had to put my hands around them in order to hold my legs down. I stared at the window of the service station. When James pointed the gun at the clerk and demanded the money, I could see the fear on the face of the skinny, white, middle-aged male attendant. My mind was screaming at me to get the hell out of there, pronto! But my ego wouldn't let my foot mash the gas pedal.

I couldn't let the guys know I was afraid. After what seemed like an hour, they came running out, jumped into the car, and I sped away like a race car driver.

As we got farther and farther away from the gas station, they all started laughing loud and talking at the same time. So many words flew around in the car that I couldn't make them all out. I heard things like "Man, that white dude was scared shitless!"; "Why didn't you steal his watch?"; and "Man, you said my name out loud!" They laughed extra hard at the way they had made the attendant find a bag to put the stolen cash in.

It wasn't really funny. It reminded me of when your mama used to make you get your own switch for your "ass-whooping'". I nervously laughed right along with the guys and congratulated them for not making any mistakes. I was relieved that they hadn't hurt the poor man and I hoped they hadn't heard my voice vibrating from fear.

Back at the apartment when we counted our "reward," we saw how easy it was to get money and not have to work for it. Hey, to us, it was fun-like in the movies.

We pulled four more robberies at service stations on the outskirts of Philly, and got enough cash for them to buy some of the flashy clothes we'd only dreamed of wearing. Our new clothes and big spending earned us a reputation in the neighborhood like the mob had in the movies. None of the attendants at the stations tried to resist us or tried to be heroes. We joked that they probably believed what they'd heard; that all black people are bad and will kill white people if given any kind of excuse. Thank God for us that wasn't true.

Soon greed took over and we wanted more money .than the service stations had to offer. One day we heard on the news that some men who had robbed an armored Brink's® truck had gotten away with millions of dollars. We knew we didn't have the expertise to do something that big; but one of the guys mentioned seeing this finance company in Chester, where his aunt lived. He thought it would be an easy mark. As we began talking about it more and more, and as the gears of a plot started to turn in our heads, we decided to get serious and check it out.

For the next two weeks we made the thirty-minute drive to Chester, Pennsylvania, to stake out the Homeland Finance Company. The neighborhood was middle class and multicultural. That fact worked in our favor; our dark skin wouldn't draw attention.

The red brick building of the finance company was located on the corner of a street that also had on it a grocery store, a car repair shop, and a few one-story apartment buildings. The main entrance to the building consisted of two huge plate-glass windows and double glass doors that led inside to a long teller-type counter.

Behind the counter were four wooden, petitioned-off desks and a huge walk-in safe located against the back wall.

We would sit in our parked car across the street from the building pretending to read a map in case we were being observed. From our vantage point we could see all the way to the back of the building. We needed to find out how many people worked there, what time they arrived at work, and how much customer activity went on throughout the day. We also wanted to know whether all of the employees went to lunch at the same time and whether or not the safe was left unlocked during the day.

When all of the necessary data was collected, we determined that a Thursday was the best day to make our move. Only two people worked that day, and the safe was always left unlocked. We would strike at noon; during lunch hour, the street was practically deserted.

Everything worked according to plan. The guys entered the building, showed them the gun, announced their intentions, tied up the two employees, took the cash from the open walk-in safe, and we made a smooth escape. Just like Ma Barker and the boys!

We drove back to Fat, Marvin's apartment, and counted the money. We had gotten away with almost $4,000, a lot of money back in the 60s! We felt like we were on the same level as Ma Barker and the boys.

I never thought about what I was doing. I justified it in my mind by convincing myself that if white folks can do it, it must be okay. The only thing we saw black actors doing was tap dancing and saying "yas suh." Blame it on my youth. Had we been wise enough to use our intelligence for forming corporations, our wealth would have been endless. It wasn't until I became grown and living on the other side of this madness that I did finally understand the magnitude of my actions. I remember saying, Why me? Why can't I park my car without it being stolen? Why did they hit my house for the third time? It took years for me to realize what I put out there in the universe was simply coming back. I do remember the voice I heard that said, Now you know how the people felt when you stole their cars! During those years of madness it was just a way of life.

We lived like millionaires for about two months ... before the money ran out. The guys were spending like crazy trying to impress the 'women in the neighborhood. I'd been wise enough to save the money I needed in order to rent the one-bedroom, furnished apartment I'd seen next door to where Fat Marvin lived. I told my grandmother that I'd inform my parents I was on my own. Of course I didn't, since I knew there was no way they were going to go for that.

We immediately started planning our next move: hitting another finance company in New Jersey. Then our luck ran out.

It had snowed especially hard on that particular November day. The guys and I were on our way back to the apartment when the car got stuck in the snow. We were right in front of a gas station, and while we were trying to dig the car out of the snow, James decided to take advantage of the situation. Without telling us, he went into the station and pulled a gun on the owner, demanding money. The owner, who was in no mood to be a victim, pulled out his gun and shot James in the neck.

We'd been digging snow with our frozen hands for about fifteen minutes and no one had noticed that James was missing. We had just gotten the car unstuck from the snow when James came running out of the station. He was bleeding badly and scared that he was dying. None of us had ever seen a real gunshot wound before. It looked as if his skin had been cut with a can opener, and dark, red blood was pumping like water out of a fire hose. It sprayed all over our clothes, and we all freaked! Nobody knew what had happened, but we knew we needed to get the hell out of there-and fast!

Though it was dear to all of us that he needed to get to the hospital, Billy pointed out that if we went inside with him, they'd want us to tell them what had happened to him; so we dropped him off at the emergency entrance, with a stiff warning: "James, you better not tell anybody what you done!" We saw the fear in his eyes, but we knew James was tough; he wouldn't rat on us.

We watched as he stumbled through the hospital doors and collapsed. I had the gas pedal to the floor before he finished falling; we shot out of there like a comet.

Of course, all it took was for the doctor to tell James that he would

Don't Blame The Road

let him bleed to death if he didn't explain to him how he got shot. James told him, alright, and he also went on to tell about all of our other exploits, as well as where our apartment was located.

So, within a very short time, the police rolled up and got all of us. Before taking us out in handcuffs, they searched the apartment for the gun. Big Marvin had hidden the gun on top of the burner in the oven of the stove and they didn't find it.

If I thought my knees had been in trouble with our first robbery, they were worse then! The police had to practically carry me to the police car in order to take me to jail, because I was so scared I couldn't make my legs move.

During the drive to the city jail, one of the officers looked at me with compassion and said, "I hate to do this to you, little girl, but you broke the law." Irene, the girlfriend of one of the guys, was arrested along with us. I felt sorry for her because she knew nothing of what was going on. I felt sorry for myself, too. I cried so hard that I knew the handcuffs I had around my wrist would rust.

Within a few days, my partners in crime managed to get bailed out by their parents. I, on the other hand, got stuck sitting in that Philly jail because my parents lived in New Jersey. And I wasn't about to call and drop the news on them that they were now raising a jailbird. To make sure the authorities didn't contact my parents, I told the police that they were dead; and truly, if they did find out where I was, I'd be dead. I'd never heard of anyone in my family ever going to jail.

Looking back at it now, my life up to that point had been one big piece of ugly-ass cake, iced over with stupidity!

I was so far into fantasy land I wasn't concerned at all about being in jail. Nor about losing my very first apartment. I just knew in my guts that my "ace boon coons in the hole" (my best friends) would get me out.

After one week went by, I was going crazy in my cell trying to understand what was-or wasn't-going on. I finally found out when Michelle, one of James's girlfriends, came to see me. She said that after bailing Irene out of jail, her parents had put her out.

Michelle was upset that the guys weren't helping her. She believed they were doing me dirty by not bailing me out, and wanted to tell me what kind of people they really were. She said they'd been bragging about getting out on bail before their prior arrests were discovered. Whenever she had asked them "When are you going to get Rose out?" they ignored the question. I couldn't believe what she was saying. After all, she was angry with James. I was confident that the guys had a plan to rescue me.

The days passed, and not one of my "aces" came forward to bail me out. Michelle was right. They had scraped me off the way people get rid of dog-doo from their shoes. There I was, abandoned once again. I had the misconception that in their eyes I was different than the women they threw aside. I wasn't feeling sorry for myself; I was blow-torch angry. I had thought these guys were my brothers!

The court date was scheduled for within thirty days of our arrest, but none of the guys showed up for the trial. That news inflamed me like a jalapeño pepper. I was anxiously waiting our day in court because I wanted to look into their faces to see if I could recognize any remorse for kicking me to the curb.

I couldn't make bail and was sent back to jail with a CFN (continued further notice). Soon the guys were picked up on their outstanding warrants, and we were all standing in court within a month. They each faced Judge Nelson with a look of "been there, done that."

We were told by our public defender not to talk at all. I'm sure that this advice served as a good reason for my "friends" to avoid looking in my direction.

Big Marvin and Slim were' sentenced to up to fifteen years in prison, which included the remainder of probation and parole time. Because they cooperated with the judge, the others were given probation.

The robbery charge was my first and only criminal offense. None of the victims involved was able to identify me as being a part of the gang, since I had always driven the getaway car. When the judge asked me who actually committed the robbery, I refused to answer. I was operating under the false code of honor-you don't rat on your friends. Because of my silence, I was given a two-year sentence. If I had responded honestly, I would have simply gotten probation.

So, why in the world did I still believe those guys were my friends? Looking back, I think I just had to feel I belonged to something or someone. They were the closest thing I had to a family, dysfunctional or not, and you never rat out family.

The strange thing was, in my mind, the biggest problem I faced was not serving a two-year sentence; instead I wondered how I was going to tell my mother and father that I was being sent to prison. In my foolish head, I was so sure that it would be out real soon, and they'd never have to know.

To complicate matters, my grandmother died shortly after I was sent to prison. When my cousin Bertha came to visit, she told me my parents were in Philadelphia making funeral arrangements. I begged her not to tell them where I was and, indeed, she promised she wouldn't. But Bertha warned me that it would only be a matter of time before they found out. I found out later that somehow she managed to convince them I was out of town.

I forced myself to fit into the routine of prison life. All I wanted was to do my time, get out, and start my life over. I spent a lot of sleepless nights in my cell. Being in prison was different than hearing about it. Not only was it degrading, it seeped way down into the core of my being. Newly arrived inmates were referred to as "new meat." This meant that everybody would take a bite out of your ass with any con game they could think 0£

If you weren't lucky enough to have somebody send you money to buy what the prison didn't supply-oftentimes, soap and toothpaste-you were forced to barter for what you needed.

Bartering consisted of cleaning cells, washing clothes, or whatever else the inmate had in mind.

I met a girl there named Lorraine, whose only crime was that she was an orphan. Never having been adopted, she had grown up in the system. When she turned eighteen, rather than put her out on the streets, they put her in prison. The only family she had were the inmates who passed her around like they would meat from a roasted pig. And because she was mentally slow, they took advantage of her body. She had scrubbed so many cells that her hair reeked of Lysol.

The incessant sounds of screaming and wailing hit my ears and penetrated down into my bones. I had to learn to find my own peace and quiet. My "private" toilet duties were performed in front of fellow prisoners, since the bare commode was positioned in the middle of the cell.

The food was bland, with hardly a trace of salt, pepper or other seasoning, and sometimes it was two days old. Other inmates told me that our food was a collection of the leftovers from the hospitals we made caps and gowns for. In the beginning, I'd often give it away even though my stomach was growling from hunger.

Like everybody else, though, I soon learned to eat it in order to survive.

Before being assigned a work detail you're confined to your wing. I was afraid to mingle, so I sat and observed my surroundings. I watched a young girl bite chucks of flesh from her arm and tear the hair from her scalp, as she wallowed in her own vomit, going through the withdrawal associated with kicking her drug habit. The seasoned inmates walked past her cell as though it was just a movie they'd seen many times before.

When the "bull daggers" (lesbians) tried to seduce me, they offered protection and some of the "good" food the staff was given. Lucky for me I didn't need their unwanted favors; I had my cousin Bertha to bring me money. You could buy a lot of things in jail for ten dollars.

When I rejected their sexual advances, they became physical. It was a reality I simply had to face up to.

On Sunday afternoons, the cells on both tiers were empty because of free time. On one of my first Sunday afternoons there, I was lying on my bunk thinking about freedom, when an inmate who had vowed to make me hers, tiptoed up and tried to kiss me. Her actions caught me off guard and it took a minute for me to gain my composure. And then the battle was on! I fought like Muhammad Ali to keep her away from me. One thing I finally knew for sure, my being gay was no longer an issue. We both ended up with a week in solitary, referred to in prison language as "the bing." Fighting was not allowed, no matter the reason. We did our time in the bing, and kept our distance from each other when we got out. Thank God, the word got around to the other "girl-men" that I was a fighter, and they wisely decided to leave me alone.

If there was a good side to being in prison, it allowed me to meet many smart and talented women. Most of them were just like me, guilty of being foolish and naive. No one openly talked about why they were in prison, but eventually the human need for comfort, or bad news from a loved one, would push the reason out of their broken souls.

We all shared the same false belief that someone else had been responsible for putting us at the gate of purgatory. We didn't seem to understand that our misguided souls led us to believe that the only way out of our grief was further destruction. The harsh regimented days and lock-down nights we earned as a result of our stupidity seemed endless.

Late into the night, I'd sit on the thin mattress of my iron bunk bed, hug my knees tight to my chest, and crawl into my thoughts.

For the first time in my life, I had plenty of time to think. Trying to ignite the light within me, which I knew was necessary to brighten my understanding of life, proved to be as difficult as graduating cum laude from Harvard University without ever having gone to elementary or high school. When you don't have access to distractions such as television or radio, you're forced to tune into yourself, causing your level of understanding to increase significantly. I was able to tap into a spiritual side of myself I had never experienced before. I thought about my father, teaching his Sunday school class and trying his best to get us young folks to understand the importance of prayer. He would say, "Stay connected to your source or you will go astray. And prayer is the only way to stay connected."

Looking at the dark gray ceiling in my cell made me realize that I really had never noticed the deep blue color of the sky, or how the cotton white clouds move so slowly, that you have to stare hard to see the motion. My mind was working overtime trying to remember the colors in the sun as it rose in the east to start a new day. For the first time I noticed the grace and freedom of birds flapping their multicolored wings that took them high up into the sky. Although my eyes beheld their image before, I never really saw them.

I hadn't recognized the beauty in them because I couldn't see it in myself Discovering the low opinion I had of myself was the hardest thing to accept. It wasn't easy to face; my life situation stared long and hard back at me every time I looked in its mirror. Up to that point I had done a lot of thinking yet very little praying. But I had found the spark I needed. The light of understanding in me wasn't shining to its full brightness, and I wasn't aware of what I was doing at the time, but I later realized I was using that time to rebuild my soul and my spirit.

A few months into my sentence, the warden sent for me-and when that happens, it's never good news. So I ran the day's events through my mind and tried to figure out what it was I must have done.

When I walked into her office, the warden asked me to have a seat. Her next words caused me to look at her with distrust. I knew that sometimes the staff would play cruel jokes on the inmates, just to watch their reactions when they discovered the truth. I figured that this was one of those pranks.

"Rose," she said, "I've been watching you. I don't know if your parents are dead or not, but I've been the warden here for a long time, and I know the people who belong here and the people who don't. Someone has done a good job raising you to do what is right. I have never done this before, but I have asked the judge to let you do the remainder of your sentence on parole. Which means you will be 'walking the gate' in a few days."

I began to take this in and tentatively let myself feel the elation of my possibly going home.

She suddenly drew up a look on her face of absolute sincerity and conviction, and said, "But if I ever see you back here again, I will act as if I don't know who you are."

Man, I wanted to kiss that stern-looking white lady! I couldn't believe what I was hearing! Although my body felt charged with the electricity of Niagara Falls, I sat there like a block of cement. I stared deeply into her green eyes, looking for a sign of truth. The tone of her voice conveyed to my soul that she was serious.

I told her she would never have to worry about seeing me again. I wouldn't even come back to visit the inmates I'd considered as my newfound friends. After serving only six months of a two-year sentence, I was set free.

I've come to accept that I had to experience the difficult situation of being locked up in prison in order for me to grow spiritually. Being incarcerated, for me, was like being paralyzed from the neck down; it was as if I was only able to move my eyes and my head. I slowly realized, though, that my mind could take me anywhere I desired to go. I imagined I was free, and in control of where I went, what food I ate, or what kind of clothes I wore.

Taking control of my thoughts gave me joy as I worked my way through a hell of a mess.

Chapter 5

Road Under Construction
"From Prison to Prosperity"

Walking to the gate was not urgent enough, I ran to it! I felt as if I could ride home on the cloud I was on. But I quickly came to my senses and caught the trolley back into town. I spent the hour-long trolley car ride trying to figure out how I was going to change my life. The self-confidence I felt before being set free was trying to divorce me. I wasn't sure if I was strong enough to resist temptation, sensing that if I went back to hanging around in my old neighborhood, I would eventually end up back in prison.

Most of my old hangout buddies were still serving time. However, there's always somebody ready and willing to show you the con game way of discovering easy money. Just the thought of that motivated me to find somewhere else to spend my time.

Later that day I rented a room from Miss Ida, a woman who ran a neighborhood boarding house. She was also the mother of my friend Beulah, and she agreed to let me pay her after I got a job. Miss Ida was known throughout the community as Mom. Right now she was the only one I had and I was determined to show her I was serious about going straight.

Within a week I was hired as a nurse's aide at Pennsylvania Hospital. I felt like I must have felt when I learned to walk on my own. Words I once heard in church flashed by my memory: "If you make one step, the Lord will help you make the others." Well, I was prepared to wear my feet out.

The two hardest times for me were in the evenings, when I'd get off from work, and the long boring weekends. Since I was keeping my distance from my old associates, I had nowhere to go and nobody to talk to.

To pass the time I began taking trolley rides from one end of the line to the other. These exploration rides gave me the opportunity to check out the nightclub scene and see different places to go to meet people, and to think.

My thoughts were always the same. How can I make it on my own? What am I going to do without the only friends I thought I had? What if I'm fired from my job when they find out about my past? Should I call my parents and tell them what happened to me? Will they reject me again? Maybe I should let them continue to think I'm lost somewhere out of town. I was one wired-up sister. I understood what Billie Holiday was trying to convey when she sang "Good Morning, Heartache."

One day during one of my rides, I happened to look up and see someone I recognized paying his fare. Cal saw me right about the same time, came over, and sat down next to me. I covertly checked him out as he sat down. The tan, thickly knit turtleneck sweater he wore hung seductively over his slender muscular body. His heat-processed hairdo and razor-sharp mustache gave him that Hollywood look; man, was he looking good! We hadn't seen each other since I'd left my grandmother's house. Our lives had gone in different directions. The kind of people I'd chosen to hang around with were not the kind of people Cal would want to know.

Breathing in his Old Spice cologne, I realized how long it was since I had been this close to a man.

"What a coincidence," he said, "I'm only riding this trolley because my car broke down. I'm on my way to rehearsal and didn't want to be late, so I decided to take the trolley."

My whole body perked up when I heard the word "rehearsal." I knew Cal was one helluva singer and I'd always loved music.

"Would you mind my tagging along, Cal?"

"I'd be more than thrilled," he replied with a look of good fortune in his eye. I was evidently looking good too!

This was turning out to be my kind of day. Not only would I have something to do, I'd have the opportunity to make new friends.

Cal was the leader of the Challengers, a fantastic rhythm and blues group. Cal played the guitar and had a smooth, sexy singing voice, like Marvin Gaye. Sara, the only girl in the group, also sang, and played the piano. Billy, was the drummer with a funky beat. Kenny played the bass, handsome Shawn was the lead vocalist, and everybody in the group sang background vocals.

What made them special was that they not only sang and played their own instruments, but also switched and played each other's. They had a rich, soulful sound with harmonies so tight, it seemed like you were hearing another voice beyond their individual voices. The beautiful music they made swept through me like the A train in a New York subway.

With so much talent and soul present in their group, they were putting together an electrifying show for future bookings. Since Cal was the one who brought me there, everyone accepted me immediately as a friend.

After the rehearsal, when the band was just fooling around, Cal asked if I would sing a few songs with them. I'd never been exposed to performing secular music before; I'd only sung spirituals with the church choir. However, I threw my head back with the confidence of a pro, opened my mouth, and crooned "Dr. Feel Good," a popular Aretha Franklin song.

I felt like I was among old friends, and asked them if I could come to the rehearsal scheduled for the next day. They all agreed, saying they'd be happy to have me.

I had found friends and a new direction in life. I decided not to tell them of my past. I was happy they hadn't known any of my former associates. I loved being involved with music again. The band only talked about doing positive things with their lives. Sharing in the construction of their dreams provided the building blocks I needed for my own. I ended up going to so many of their rehearsals that I learned the whole show, choreography, songs and all.

Sara had written a song called "One Heart to Break Over You." My eyes turned into waterfalls every time she sang it, and I begged her to teach it to me. I was too bashful to sing in front of other people, so I would only perform around the members of the band. Whenever Cal and I sang together, I'd pretend we were Marvin Gaye and Tammi Terrell, top duet singers for Motown.

When the group started to get bookings, I was right out there with the audience, cheering them on. I followed them everywhere they went. Soon, some of the more upscale Philadelphia dubs started to book the group.

Every dub they played had standing room only crowds, and I felt privileged to know the group intimately. I also felt special when I didn't have to pay for tickets and got front row seats.

Their big break came when a big-time talent scout for exclusive dubs from New York to L.A.. heard them one night and offered them a contract; without much hesitation they all gratefully accepted.

Soon they were appearing at five-star dubs like The Latin Casino right outside of Philadelphia, and Club Harlem in Atlantic City, New Jersey. The Challengers had risen to the stature of being the opening act for big-name groups like The O'Jays, The Delfonics, Chubby Checker, and the like. They were making more money than they had ever seen.

Cal and I had become an "item" by now, so I was able to travel along with the group in their custom Chevy van, being part of a very "happening" music scene. I knew I must have been doing something right in trying to change my life. Here I was, a former prisoner, sitting backstage in the dressing room of all these famous people. I couldn't believe my good fortune!

I would periodically be incited by my ego to look up old friends and execute my bragging rights about the "who's who" I now had for friends. However, keeping pace with the group forced me to put that moment of triumph on hold.

In the midst of all this activity and fanfare, something happened that was to take my life in yet another direction.

One night, Sara became violently ill with a severe case of the flu and laryngitis. She was able to play the piano but when she opened her mouth to sing, nothing came out. She tried screaming like James Brown, but the only sound we heard from her was a weak whisper.

When she returned from visiting her doctor, she announced the bad news to us, saying she would be out of commission .for at least two weeks. That would mean the group would have to drop out of the remainder of the tour. They knew if that happened, chances of their getting back on the musical circuit would be slim. With so many talented people in the entertainment business, you had to stay visible or you were quickly forgotten.

Since I was the only one who knew the routine and the songs, the group began pressuring me. "You just have to fill in for Sara, Rose!", they urged.

I was petrified and couldn't imagine myself singing and dancing in front of hundreds of people! I knew I would probably drop dead as soon as the curtain went up. Besides, I was afraid that someone in the audience might recognize me and tell my parents their choir-singing daughter was now a night dub rhythm and blues singer. Or worse, the warden would see the show and want to come backstage to congratulate me. My secret would be blown.

Eventually, after some real soul-searching, I realized I had to swallow my fears and help my desperate friends. We rehearse all day getting ready for that night's show. I prayed and did my mental exercises to convince myself: "I can do it." I felt like I was doing okay ... until I stepped out onto the stage of The Wonder Gardens in Atlantic City.

It was as large as a football field, with what seemed to be a thousand lights shining right on me. Those lights were so bright that I couldn't see the audience. I'd never seen the stage from this angle before and I froze up. The only things moving were my knees. They were shaking so hard I thought I was, going to fall down.

When the band began playing the intro music to the song that I was to open with, I was so petrified that I couldn't remember any of the words. The introduction came and went a second time, and I was still standing there, frozen! Cal saw what was happening and strolled over to me, pretending that it was all a part of the act. He began to tell me the words to the song. The thunderous applause at the end of that song made me feel as if I 'just might get through the night.

I was finally able to relax halfway through the show, and in the end we got a standing ovation.

The audience loved us, and The Challengers' talent agent, Earl, wanted to sign me up immediately as a permanent member of the group. All I could think about was, only a few months ago I was sitting in prison, trying to figure out what I was going to do with my life, and here I was, beginning to prosper. I had made some good friends and was going to be paid a lot of money to sing.

Webster's dictionary says the definition for the word "roadblock" is an obstruction in the road; any hindrance or obstacle. What it doesn't say, though, is there's always a way around any obstacle. Jumping over the high hurdle of my fears helped create the life I wanted.

Rose Bilal as Harriett Tubman

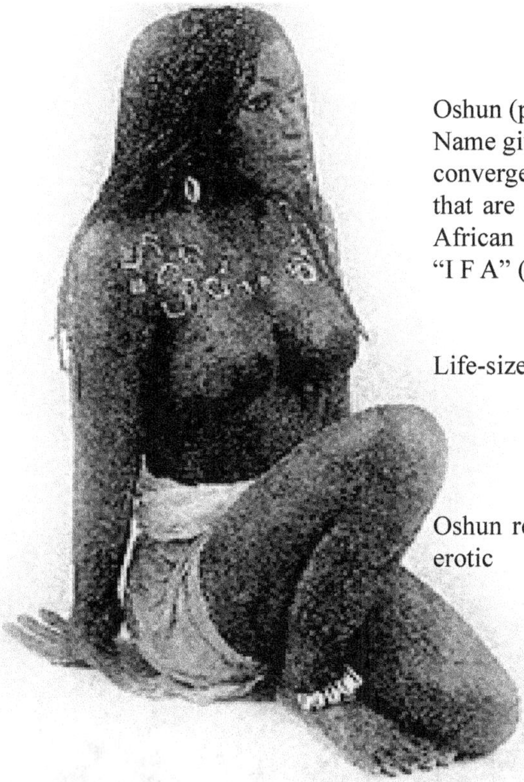

Don't Blame The Road

Oshun (pronounced - o'shoon) Name given to describe a complex convergence of spiritual forces that are key elements in the west African religious tradition called "I F A" (e'fah).

Life-size paper mache

Oshun represents fertility and the erotic

Chapter 6

Flat Tire Blues
"Giving Up My Freedom Again"

Intoxicated with the idea of traveling full time with the band, I couldn't suffer through my job's required two-week notice of leave; I simply left. Miss Ida and Beulah both thought I was making a huge mistake, and loudly told me so. I don't think they really understood the difference between a gang and a band.

Everything was happening so fast in my life, and I wasn't taking the time to really think things through. While I had walked down the path of crime, Cal had walked down the aisle of marriage. They promptly had five children, which included twins. He said their marriage had ended a few years earlier because she couldn't accept him wanting to make music a career. I never asked his wife if those facts were correct; I believed every word he said. The fast-paced world I was propelled into didn't encourage rational thinking.

During our breaks from the road, the band would rehearse at Cal's house. Most nights he didn't want me to go home and would beg me to stay. I would give in to his pleas because I wanted to and would end up spending the night. One night turned into two and before I knew it, I was doing something I hadn't planned on, and something I knew my parents would never approve 0£ I was living with a man without being married.

But I was having so much fun, I didn't care what anybody thought. Or so I wanted to believe. In my heart I knew I still longed for my parents' love and approval. I wanted them to know that I was back in Philly and doing okay, but I was afraid they'd want to come for a visit.

I made myself believe that once I told my mom and dad about everything I'd been through, and how I was now trying to change my life for the better, they would understand. I figured I'd tell them that Cal was helping me stay out of trouble by letting me hang out with his group. I'd hoped that they would be grateful to him for his helping to "save me," and not angry about my living with him. I knew I was lying to myself, just like I was lying to myself about what was really going on in our relationship.

Things between us actually started to change as soon as I became a member of the band. Although he'd pleaded as hard as the rest of the group for me to come on board, he seemed to resent the attention I was getting from the audience, especially the men.

At first it felt good to have him become jealous about me. I was naive enough to believe that it meant he loved me. But it soon stopped being fun and I began feeling more like a prisoner. I began to move into the depths of desolation and what was worse, I had put myself there. Trying to avoid an argument with Cal had forced me to stop calling or visiting with my girlfriends anymore, and I was afraid to give even a casual greeting to a man. I bought into Cal's theory that I was too good for my old girlfriends. After all, they dated criminals. I felt like a robot, with Cal in control of my program.

The loss of my freedom, this time, was the result of trying to accommodate the unrealistic demands of my jealous mate. I was still allowing myself to believe that I was lucky to have someone like Cal who wanted to be with me. After all, this was the guy all the women were screaming for. I tried to be everything and do everything he wanted so that he wouldn't reject me. What I failed to grasp was the fact that I was renouncing myself.

Cal knew the things to say to trigger me into feeling like broadloom, something he could walk on. From time to time he would drop subtle suggestions about my friend Beulah, or any woman that I chose as a close friend, that something was wrong with them. He was implying that they were gay. He knew I was very sensitive about that issue and his remarks would eventually cause me to end the friendship. That always made him happy.

There were times, after a performance, when I felt forced to explain that the guy I'd dedicated a song to was just someone in the audience and not someone I knew personally. One day, Cal went into a, "throwing things around" rage when he came home and found his brother, Melvin, waiting for him. He said, "I don't want any men in my house when I'm not at home." It did not matter to him that this was his brother.

By the time I finally decided to make contact with my family, I allowed myself to be kept away with excuses of our not having enough time to go to New Jersey for a visit. I knew that wasn't true because we always made time for whatever he wanted to do.

When you don't want to change the things you are doing in your life, it's easy to cover up what you know to be the true nature of a person.

I noticed that Cal always had to have total control of the lives of the people around him. He would lie if it suited him or got him what he wanted. He deliberately used the people who were supposed to be his friends. Sometimes he was downright nasty to them. Everybody in the group made excuses for his behavior because they didn't want to face reality either.

But I told myself, He'd never treat me that way because he loves me.

I wasn't smart enough, nor did I want to face the fact that this was the kind of person Cal was. So I made up excuses and looked the other way when the negative things I didn't like about him surfaced.

I didn't want to deal with the realities of life, so I ignored the truths of my relationship with Cal; I thought it would be easier that way and would allow me to hold onto this new and exciting way of life. I perfected my "entertainer's smile" and ignored my fractured heart.

I loved the boost my singing with the group gave my professional career, yet I was beginning to be extremely unhappy with the way things were going in my personal life. I would blame myself for the control Cal had over me, but then I'd turn around and try harder to please him. I wanted to fit into whatever mold he made for me, just to keep the peace. Maybe I still wanted to believe he was the best thing to happen to me.

Sometimes after a show, I would be drained and want to go back to the hotel to rest. Cal would insist on my hanging out with him and the group to go partying. It didn't matter how hard I protested, he pretended not to hear. I was expected to go along with him, and if he saw that I wasn't having a good time, we'd get into a big fight about how my attitude made him look bad in front of his friends. I would actually try to figure out what I kept doing wrong to upset him. I found myself walking quietly around, trying hard to do whatever he wanted.

The part of my being that rejected his behavior would prompt me to deliberately do things I knew would give him grief. I would sneak a phone call to my parents and make sure he found out about it. This made him angry; he knew they didn't care for me living with him and that they wanted me to leave him.

Cal had a bad habit of borrowing things from friends but never returning the items. He'd go so far as to lie about the fact that he had borrowed something or he'd make up stories about having lost it. I would quietly return the items to their owners and tell them he had lied. They were shocked to find out how far he'd go to have his way. Even so, they were still afraid to confront him about his actions.

Of course I caught hell when he found out I'd given it back to them and he would scream about it for hours. I would drop my head and secretly smile to myself. It did my heart good to give him some of the grief he handed out without feeling. I can only imagine the hell his ex-wife and children must have endured.

I tried explaining to the rest of the group how miserable Cal was making my life and I didn't know how much longer I was going to take it. They'd beg and plead with me not to leave him. Having become accustomed to living this great lifestyle, they didn't want it to stop. Once again, it seemed I was going out of my way to please other people, even at the expense of my own freedom. And so, for the sake of the group, I ended up staying with him longer.

As time passed, I got the feeling I was living my life only for Cal and the group. That feeling stayed with me for the next two years, until one day I'd finally had enough. I had to take back control of my own life. A newfound strength prompted me to go to Cal to get him to talk openly and honestly about our relationship. I told him that I no longer had the kind of feelings for him that were necessary for a relationship to work. I said I was no longer willing to be dominated and controlled. However, I also expressed to him that I wanted to remain his friend, and I wanted to remain in the group until we finished our contract, which would end in six months.

I knew from the way he spoke and from the cold expression on his face, that he meant every word he said: "I don't care if you love me or not. But if you ever try to leave me, I'll kill you."

There was no doubt in my mind that he was capable of murder and would not hesitate to do just that.

Now that he'd threatened my life, I was more determined than ever to get out. He knew I was serious about leaving and he knew it would be almost impossible for me to start over without money. He began holding back my pay while he paid the rest of the group. I'd always hand over my check to him for the household, so I didn't understand the gesture. He warned the other members that they would have to answer to him if he ever found out that they'd given me any money.

I told them not to bring his wrath on themselves by trying to help me, but I advised them that they needed to secretly look for and train another singer because I was going to leave. I knew that, somehow, I'd find a way to gain my freedom again.

The inner connection I'd made while sitting in my cell was strongly compelling me to fight. I realized that it was my choice as to how I had allowed myself to be treated. I chose to no longer accept Cal's abuse. I took a mental inventory of everything I'd lose by leaving the relationship: money, notoriety, designer clothes, newly remodeled house, and my red Cadillac.

I realized that the only thing of any real value to me now was courage.' I had always thought that if I had enough money, I would be happy; but I found out nothing is further from the truth. For the first time in my life, I understood what rich people meant when they said "Money won't buy you happiness." There I was making a lot of money, living in a showcase home/wearing the latest designer clothes, driving a brand-new car. I had everything money could buy; and yet I was a very unhappy person.

Chapter 7

One Way Out
"Breaking Free"

Revealing my true feelings to Cal made me even more of a prisoner because then he began to watch my every move. He never left me alone with anybody long enough for me to ask them for money or to help me in any way.

I couldn't bring myself to have sex with him anymore. His touch repulsed me and my mouth would fill with saliva, like when you have to vomit. Whenever he became frustrated about that fact, he wrestled me down and raped me. Those were the worst times. It would have been better if a strange had raped me because I wouldn't have to look at him in the morning. Things seemed only to be getting worse.

The group was back in Philly for the two-week break in between shows. My family was getting together for an annual family reunion that was being held in Philadelphia that year. Cal didn't feel comfortable being around my family, so he didn't want to go. He knew that if I went by myself, I would be able to get someone to help me leave him; so he forbade me to go. I hadn't seen my family in a long time and I was determined to go.

We got into a heated argument and he slapped me so hard my eyeballs went out of control. I was afraid he was going to kill me; all I could think about was getting away. I began hitting him with all the strength I could find in me. He wasn't expecting me to retaliate, so it caught him off guard. He grabbed my hands and tried to protect himself We wrestled for a few minutes and then he started to laugh. It was funny to him that I actually thought I could beat him up. After he calmed me down, he tried to apologize to me and swore he'd never hit me again.

I remember very dearly saying to myself, I know you won't because I won't be here. I was not going to stay with him, or anyone, and take that kind of abuse.

Every day my mind was filled with thoughts of what I could do to get away from this man before I'd end up back in prison, for murder; I knew that if he ever hit me again, I would kill him. I sometimes felt as if that might be my only means of escape.

The only time I was able to be away from him was when I was allowed to go to Charlie's grocery store around the corner. I was on friendly terms with Charles, the owner of the store, and decided to ask him for help. I explained my situation and told him I wanted to use his store as a drop-off point for my clothes. I would sneak my clothes out of the house, one piece at a time, and take them to his store. My friend and former co-worker, Juanita, would then come pick them up and take them to her house. The plan was that later,

I would collect my clothes from Juanita's house after I made my escape from Cal.

One day Cal noticed some of my clothes were missing from the closet. He knew practically everything I wore or bought. I'd only been able to sneak out two of my old wool pantsuits. I told him they were in the dry cleaners. I got lucky; he didn't ask me to show him a receipt. As he turned to walk away, the blood that had frozen in my veins began to flow again. I don't even want to think what would have happened if he uncovered my plot to escape from his tight, controlling grip!

When it was time for the group to go back on the road, I was forced to put my plans on hold. This was a huge disappointment to me since I knew I wouldn't be able to endure another day of his relentless jealousy. Throughout the tour, Cal's menacing presence and insane accusations helped put more wind in the sail that would take me out of his life.

I didn't know it at the time, but shortly after returning from our road tour, the tragic death of my sister would prove to be the ticket to my freedom.

We arrived back in Philadelphia one night at about four o'clock in the morning. I'd just gotten into bed when I heard the doorbell ring. It was my uncle Walter, and he told me that my sister was in the hospital and wasn't expected to live much longer. He couldn't tell me what had happened to her because my mother had been too upset to give him that information.

...

I realized I hadn't been in touch with my sister in months. A voice deep within my heart silently questioned, How could I have let anybody erase our bond? How could I not know she needed me?

I wanted to leave right then and ride over to New Jersey with my uncle, but instead I gave in to Cal's insistence that he drive me there.

As soon as my uncle left, Cal told me he wasn't going to take me anywhere. He said, "There ain't nothing you can do for your sister, so I don't see any need for you to be there."

I stood there in silence, feeling the blood in my body reaching its boiling point. Before it spilled out of my eyes, I picked up the telephone and called my cousin Clarence. I explained to him, through clenched teeth, what was going on, and pleaded with him to take me to my parents' house. The look I had on my face told Cal that he'd better back off and leave me alone.

But when Clarence came to pick me up, Cal hopped into the car with us. He wasn't about to let me go to New Jersey by myself because he knew that if I did, I would never come back.

My mother couldn't give me much more information about why

my sister was in the hospital, dying. The friends at her apartment that night said they had no idea what caused her to pass out. I didn't know anything about my sister's friends, therefore it was difficult for me to know if they were telling the truth.

I sat by my sister's hospital bed squeezing her hand hard so she would know I was there; The last conversation I'd had with Annette had been a few months earlier when she announced she was tired of being hurt and abused by men. She now was in love with a woman named Audrey and hoped her being a lesbian wouldn't keep me from loving her. I assured her that would never happen. I only hoped she believed me.

I prayed day and night asking God to spare her young life. I longed for the chance to talk with her again. But that wasn't to be.

Annette lingered in a coma for two weeks before she died. The autopsy revealed the cause of death was an overdose of sleeping pills and some kind of poison she had taken. The doctor said that the poison could have been the result of combining alcohol with the sleeping pills. It really was mysterious to us, because my sister didn't drink or take pills. It went against her formula of being a good mother.

I understood my sister's pain but could not accept the fact that she chose death as the only way out of her prison.

Every single day of those two weeks in New Jersey, Cal made my life a living hell. I refused to disrespect my parents in their home by sleeping in the same room with him, as we weren't married. That made him furious. He didn't understand my thinking because by now my parents knew I was living with him. I tried to explain to him that there was a difference between being in our house and being at my parents' house. Besides, I knew my mother would never allow us to sleep together.

He angrily disagreed with my reasoning, and said I was only doing it because I was trying to turn my parents against him. Since I felt I didn't need this added stress, especially when dealing with my sister's death, I tried, but to no avail, to get him to go home. My insistence only angered him and brought more of his whispered threats in my ear. There was still more for me to do to gain my freedom.

I'll never forget that cold February day when my sister's body was lowered into the snow-covered ground. My memory began to rewind to the times of joy and sorrow Annette and I had shared together. I stood there with tears frozen on my face, thinking, I really didn't know her at all. I had been sent to live in Philly just at the time we were becoming close.

While standing there reminiscing about Annette, I sensed Cal moving closer to me, and in a low, chilling voice he said, "I hope you don't plan on going back to your parents' house with your family. Ain't nothing else you can do for your sister and I'm ready for us to go home." In spite of everything he had done to me, it was clear this was the first time I felt genuine hatred for him. I felt he was totally evil, with no compassion for anyone.

As he continued whispering his threats, I said in the loudest voice e I could muster, that he was to "Leave me alone!" My muscular male cousins heard me arguing with him and came over to help. I told them I was okay, and I was going to ride back to the house with them. Cal knew better than to try and stop me; it was obvious my cousins would have stomped all the evil out him, or at least tried their best.

Cal's craziness didn't take away the contentment I felt from being with my family again. My aunt Frances, who lived in Tampa, Florida, was chatting with me about our families' not keeping in touch with each other. I briefly told her what was going on with me, and how desperate I was to change my location. She suggested I come live with her and my uncle Charlie until I could put my life in order.

I gratefully accepted her invitation and begged her not to tell my parents about my plans. I knew Cal was devious enough to use tears and other theatrical tricks as a means to get information from my mother about my whereabouts. I remembered his threat to kill me if I ever tried to leave him. Still, I was doing just that.

I told Cal I was going to spend the rest of the day with my family and I'd catch a train later that night to New Jersey. We had a show to do at the Elks home in New Brunswick. I watched him cringe at the idea of leaving me behind, but knew he couldn't force me to go with him. My aim was to be on the plane with Aunt Frances and Uncle Charlie when they left for Florida the next day.

As soon as Cal left, I went to work making my plan a reality. I needed money to live on so that I wouldn't be totally dependent on my aunt and uncle. I approached Uncle Isaiah, who listened quietly as I explained my need to get out of a bad situation ... and I asked for his financial help. I told him my wish was to get a job and return to school to complete my education. I'd start to work right away and begin to pay him back as soon as I was able.

I knew my life was already changing for the better. He said, "Gal, if you are really serious about what you say and really do something to improve your life, you won't have to pay back one penny to me. But if you ever go back to that abusive man, then I want every dime of my money plus 10 percent interest!"

I promised him he would never have to worry about that because I'd learned my lessons quite well. He then said he thought it would be safer if I stayed the night with him, since Cal didn't know where he lived. I agreed, and called my friend Juanita. I explained my change of plans and thanked her for her friendship. I promised I'd be in touch with her when I was sure it was safe.

I had been forced to leave Philadelphia with, literally, the clothes on my back, and none of the money I had worked so hard to earn; but somehow none of that seemed to matter. My uncle had given me a first-class, one-way ticket to Tampa and enough money to live on for three months. My mind, body, and spirit were experiencing total peace. I was FREE once again!

And though I was consumed with fear after I thought of trying to make it on my own, at the same time I was listening to that little voice I'd discovered. It said to me, Your soul has been given the responsibility to learn the true meaning of love.

Love is such an easy word to say. It's used by millions of people, but very few really understand the true meaning of love. Love, to most of us, is defined by what we've learned from television or the movies. When we try to apply what we saw on the big screen with Brad Pitt and what's-her-name, to what really happens in life, that's when we discover it's not real. It's pure illusion. We have been programmed to have unrealistic expectations of ourselves and our mates, and, as a result of that, most of us lead unhappy lives.

I learned not to hate Cal for what I allowed him to do to me. I came to know that true love is when you can put what happened aside and pray for your mate, family or friends, and hope they find the peace and understanding we all need in order to love ourselves and pass it on to others. I loved myself enough to trust that voice that was saying I was going to be okay no matter what happens. I found the courage to remove myself from a situation that would have kept me from evolving spiritually and experiencing a joyful and fulfilling life.

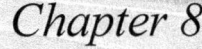

Chapter 8

Shifting Gears
"A New Life in Florida"

A*rriving* in Tampa on that beautiful Sunday afternoon in 1969 was thrilling. My mind was filled with the vision of Dr. Martin Luther King, the civil rights movement, and people singing at the top of their lungs: "FREE AT LAST, FREE AT LAST, THANK GOD ALMIGHTY, I'M FREE AT LAST!"

I had no idea what I was going to do to support myself. With little education, my job experience so far had been limited to strong-arm robbery and rhythm and blues singing. I happened to see an article in the classified section of my uncle's newspaper for a · seamstress. I thought it would be a remarkable idea to put the skill I'd picked up in prison to good use.

My Aunt Frances-Frank, as we called her-volunteered to take me to a few of the local factories to fill out applications. As luck would have it, I landed a job pretty quickly at Tropical Garment, a factory manufacturing men's pants for all the major department stores. The woman who hired me saw how fast I operated the power sewing machine and neglected to ask for past references. I suppose she thought I'd be an asset to the company. The sun was showing me how bright it could shine!

* * *

I called my parents after a few weeks to let them know I was alive and well. They told me Cal had been all over New Jersey and Philadelphia looking for me. He had called them, crying and pleading to tell him where I was. Of course they couldn't, because they didn't know. So I told them it was better that way; then they wouldn't have to tell a lie when or if he called again. I could sense the anguish Cal must have been experiencing at the thought of losing control. Although they wanted to know my whereabouts, my parents were glad I was safe, and didn't press for more information.

I would have given anything to see the look on Cal's face when he realized I had managed to get away from him, and that he hadn't a clue where to start looking for me. I had been barely allowed to keep in contact with my family. He used the excuse "that we couldn't afford the telephone bill," but his eyes held a rage that terrified me. I didn't know how crazy he would get, so I stopped calling them. The only upside was that Cal never heard me talk about my relatives in Florida, so I knew I'd be safe with them.

I was feeling pretty damn confident about myself and my ability to survive. Within just three months of my arrival in Tampa, I had a full-time job, I'd moved into my own apartment, and I was enrolled in night school to get my high school diploma.

That took me less than a year, and I graduated from George Washington Adult Night School with honors and a scholarship award for college. For the first time ever my brain felt alive. I'd always thought I was too stupid to learn. I never realized I hadn't taken the effort to shake my lazy mind awake.

After taking a few months off from school, I enrolled at the local junior college; I took mostly clerical skills courses in order to find a better paying job. I'd always dreamed of working in an office because it would enhance my self-esteem. I also hoped it would take me up a notch or two in my mother's eyes. She believed that an education and a good job were next to godliness.

Even though I had graduated from night school and was now enrolled in college, I continued to work at the pants factory. I knew I was ready to step up in life, but was afraid of being turned down by the corporate world if they should find out about my past.

My cousin Gussie, Fuzzy was her nickname, who worked for GTE, the local telephone company, kept asking me why I wouldn't come and apply to work there. No one except my criminal friends up North knew about my stay in prison. I was too ashamed and embarrassed to tell anyone about my past, so I told Fuzzy that I hadn't been able to get off from work to fill out an application.

But I knew I wouldn't be able to hide behind my fears much longer. I went through a lot trying to convince myself that I was strong enough to do it; I finally discovered my wings were for flying, and left the nest.

I felt my liver shaking as I sat there filling out the application for the phone company. I wasn't sure what I was going to write when I got to the part of the application that asked questions about one's personal life.

While filling in the answers, I realized the only question that came dose to asking if I'd ever broken the law, was the one that asked if I'd ever been bonded. I asked God to forgive me and quickly wrote "No" in the appropriate box. My limited understanding of terminology caused me to think "bonded" meant having to pay bail to get out of jail. Years later I would learn the true definition.

I passed all the required exams: data processing, communications skills, typing, etc. On February 21, 1972, I was hired as a long distance operator. I'd finally made it to the corporate world. I recall saying to myself, I will never have to work in a factory again. At least I loved my job. I got to wear nice new business suits instead of work jeans. I had my own private work area and, in no time at all I made lots of new friends. My job assignment gave me the opportunity to exercise my brain with something other than threading a needle. I learned how to operate the complicated cord board that transferred all incoming calls throughout the company. There were so many lights and cords, I thought I'd never learn; but my determination won out and I became adept at all of the telephone procedures, and even developed a way to organize my work so I could complete it faster.

I was so thrilled to have a real job that I often went above and beyond the call of duty. When something needed to be done, it didn't matter if it fell under my job classification or not; I jumped in and did it. I was always on time and ready to work. Because of my "dynamo" attitude, my co-workers would jokingly accuse me of trying to earn brownie points. It didn't bother me because I knew that they would never understand why I was so happy to be on the job.

Due to my take-charge attitude and dedication to getting the job done, one of the supervisors in my unit, Mrs. Crawford, took notice of me. It caused her to step out of her normal way of doing business, to recommend me for the position of service representative that had recently become available. This was unusual because company policy stated that an employee had to be on the job for at least one year in order to put in for a promotion. I had been at GTE for only ten months. Strangely enough, I had no idea that Mrs. Crawford had recommended me for the job.' She never mentioned it to me. In fact it was rare for her to say anything to anyone. A year later, during my evaluation, the office manager told me how Mrs. Crawford had been impressed and inspired by my work, and that it was she who had been responsible for moving me up into that position. Although I didn't realize it at the time, striving to be my best was helping to create the belief that I can make it on my own.

I transferred to the newly-opened GTE Phone Mart shortly after being promoted, and was among the first of many employees to work there. Since I'm a "people person," it was the greatest job to have. We talked with our customers face-to-face, not over the telephone. That kept my stress level very low because people are a lot nicer to you when they are not on a phone.

The way that GTE set it up, everyone who moved to Florida had to either call in or visit a phone mart in order to start telephone service; so I met people from all over the world. I loved asking applicants the question on the service application about their place of employment because it always led to an interesting conversation about their lives; and getting to ask that question was how I ended up back in the entertainment business.

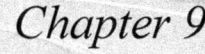

Chapter 9

Tootin' The Horn
"Something to Sign About"

I knew there was something special about him when he came into the phone mart. A tall, dark-haired, pleasant-looking white man walked past the other representatives and approached my desk. "You look like you're ready to work and I need a phone," he said.

I handed him the application and he sat down to write. When he handed it back to me, I noticed he'd written "musician" as his means of employment. I asked about his musical background, and he told me the name of his group and all the places they'd played.

As he talked, I began to feel comfortable enough to tell him about my experience as an entertainer. I could see he was very interested in what I was sharing with him.

Then he said, "God must have had a hand in the fact that you were the one I was drawn to. My brother's group is in need of a female singer because the one they currently have is going on tour for a year. Several singers have auditioned, but they're not happy with any of them. Maybe you'll be what they're looking for."

My emotions were in turmoil at the thought of getting on stage again, and I wasn't sure if I could still hold a note; I hadn't tried to sing at all since I'd left Philly.

I told him I would think about it. Before he left he told me I told him I would think about it. Before he left he told me where his brother's group was playing that night and suggested I go and listen. He was sure if I heard the great sound they had and saw how professional they were, I would definitely want to join.

For the rest of that day, my head was buzzing with little voices saying to me, You can always use the money ... but do you want to get in front of people again? Can you work during the day and perform at night? Will the guys in the group like you? What will you wear? You'll have to learn the latest songs. What about the men? They always want to date the female singer, don't they! Are you ready for that? What if they find out about your past? Will they still want you in their group?

I couldn't concentrate at all on my work and just sat there with sweaty palms, trying to make it through the day. That night something made me walk to my car and drive to the dub.

When I arrived I could tell by the way the band looked at me that they had been told all about me. It wasn't too hard to figure out I might be the one, since most of the people in the dub were white.

When they took their break, the leader of the group headed straight to my table and said, "You must be Rose. I was hoping you'd come.",,

I liked Tony right away. He was an attractive younger version of his brother, with the biggest smile and bashful nature of a little boy. Which fit right in with my little girl fear. He was eager to hear my voice and asked me to sit in on their next set.

I'd never gotten over my stage fright. My stomach felt a million butterflies were in there fighting to get out. I could feel that old familiar sensation of losing my supper. The feeling stayed with me until I finished my first song. My knees finally stopped quivering and I stood tall as the people applauded for me. For me!

After I finished singing an old Aretha Franklin number with the band, the audience clapped and shouted for more. It felt so sweet to be appreciated that I sang for the rest of the night, doing all kinds of "oldies but goodies" because they were the songs I sensed this audience could relate to. It was wonderful to see the owner of the club tapping his foot, too.

At the end of the night, the leader of the group turned to me and said, "You have a jo6, if you will do us the honor."

Hesitantly, I accepted the job and told him I would be the one honored to work with them. This was a new beginning for us as a group, so we decided to call ourselves "SOMETHING NEW"

We rehearsed every night for the next two weeks, which helped us become tight both musically and as friends-to-be.

I admit that I did spend some time experiencing flashbacks. The scenario was the same as when I had met Cal, which caused me to reflect some; but that's where the similarities ended. This time the e was no big-time recording agent and 1 wasn't romantically involved with the leader of the group.

Word got around about how good we ere and the gigs started pouring in. My life was full of everything I loved, so I couldn't understand why I felt that something was missing. Sometimes during a performance I'd find myself watching couples dancing together, looking into each other's eyes with love in their hearts. I hungered to know that kind of love. I sometimes wondered if anyone would ever really love me.

I began to realize that I had the "missing something" feeling because I was lonely. I had been so traumatized by Cal, I hadn't allowed myself to think about the possibility of being with anybody. But a series of coincidences seemed to be creating the possibility of a new relationship. And this time I was sure I knew what I wanted.

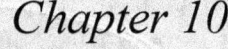

Chapter 10

Caution: Soft Shoulders
"Mixed Emotions and Good Sense"

W__hile__ my cousin Fuzzy and I were out clubbing one evening, we ran into a guy she had gone to school with. Randy was tall, very good-looking, and carried himself in a manner that said "Hey, check me out!" I hadn't seen anyone dressed that flashy since I'd left Philly. And since he reminded me of my idol, Sidney Poitier, I decided to call him Sidney.

Our eyes made contact and I was immediately in lust, which I mistook for love. He ended up spending the evening with us at Grace's Place, a favorite club for the "in crowd." Later, he asked if he could take me home. I was reluctant at first because I didn't know him well enough to know if I could trust him or not. Since I was so busy thinking about how cute he was, I hadn't bothered to learn who he really was.

My cousin assured me that Sidney was trustworthy, so I happily agreed to let him drive me home in his brand-new lemon yellow LeMans. He had all of the latest eight-track tapes and I'was surrounded by music that definitely shot my libido to the moon. But I forced myself to remain earthbound.

When he pulled into my driveway, we sat in his car and talked until the sun came up. When he walked me to my door, he made no attempt to kiss me goodnight. I gave him ten points for his being a "gentleman". When he asked if he could come in, I said "yes" so loudly that I embarrassed myself There I was trying to be a lady, but what I really wanted was to tear those fancy clothes right off his body!

We began spending every spare minute together. I could hardly wait until I got off from work so I could be with him, and he felt the same way. I was impressed with him for not putting pressure on me to have sex. I told him all about my past and the bad experience I had with my ex-mate.

He was comforting to talk to, so understanding, and I was falling deeper and deeper in love. Doing leaps and bounds, my heart flew past all of my good advice, straight to disaster.

After a few weeks of holding hands and heavy petting, I was ready to go further. I planned a romantic evening for the two of us, complete with a candlelight dinner and supermarket pink champagne. Even though I now could afford to shop elsewhere, I bought a very expensive, sexy red negligee from the Goodwill. (I still loved the surprises you could find at the Goodwill.) I seductively slipped into my "take me, I'm yours" mode. I was ready for a fun-filled evening.

I remember feeling guilty as we both drifted off to sleep, because I had pretended to enjoy myself more than I really had during our lovemaking. I actually still expected the Hollywood version ... you know, where he holds you tight and tells you how wonderful you are. But instead of violins playing, all I heard was his loud snoring!

The next morning we had an early breakfast together and went our separate ways. As I drove to work I realized he didn't say he would call me that evening. But I knew he would, because we were in love, right?

When I got off from work, I rushed home and waited for my usual evening telephone call. When I hadn't heard from him by nine o'clock, I was sure that something had happened to him.

I didn't sleep at all that night and spent a long miserable day at work the next day.

When I got home that evening he was sitting in front of my apartment. I was so happy to see him, but I was also mad at him. He told me he had been out of town on a family emergency, and that he was sorry he hadn't been able to call to let me know what had happened. Something deep inside me knew he was not telling me the truth, but I wasn't ready to listen to that voice. He spent the night and we made love, but the passion he had displayed a few nights earlier was missing.

I'd promised never to put myself into a situation where I became the victim, and that's exactly what I was doing. I had to remember that I was in control of my happiness. This man was not the reason I was unhappy.

About three weeks later, while sitting in the break room at work, I noticed a woman staring at me with hatred in her eyes. I had never seen her before and I couldn't imagine why she would be looking at me that way. She seemed to know me.

That night I felt lonely as I stretched across my bed, but I felt happy about my new furniture in my first apartment. As I looked around the room I noticed Sid's wallet wedged between the mattress and the wall. When I picked it up, some photographs fell on the floor and there, staring up at me, was the face of the woman with the hate-filled eyes. My Sid was her man too! In that instant, everything became clear.

Instead of feeling my heart being torn out of my chest, I had this incredible sensation of peace. I realized that this was the result of my bad judgment, of my not paying attention to the signs I'd been given about his not being honest.

When I saw him that evening, I made no mention of my finding the wallet because I wanted to talk with the woman in the picture before confronting him. I made an excuse of not feeling well and told him I wanted to spend the evening alone. He sensed something wasn't right but didn't waste his time pursuing it.

As fate would have it, the next morning she and I arrived at the elevator at the same time. She glared at me as I smiled and introduced myself. I told her that we needed to talk, and she reluctantly agreed to meet me for lunch at Biffy's Cafe.

I managed to get there first and when she came in, I saw something I hadn't noticed earlier that morning. She was pregnant! That revelation answered all my questions.

She wanted to be angry with me for stealing her man, but I could tell she was deeply embarrassed. I told her my story and assured her my relationship with Sid was over. I found her to be a likable person, and under different circumstances, we would have been friends.

As we went our separate ways, I silently asked God to forgive me because I hadn't been able to bring myself to tell her about the other women whose pictures I had seen. I knew she would find out for herself.

That night at the club, I returned Sid's wallet and confronted him about the woman in the photos. I wished I had an umbrella to shield me from the rain of crap that came flying out of his mouth. Had it not been a sad situation, it would have been laughable. All I could think of was, That poor little baby being born to a confused mother and a father who probably didn't want it.

I told him it was over and there was no use in his lying to me. When he left that night, I could tell he didn't take me seriously. A week later there he sat in front of my apartment, smiling. Even though I was annoyed, I spoke to him as politely as I could.

He said, "I just dropped by to see if you needed anything."

We both knew what that "anything" meant. I reminded him that I wasn't the one who was pregnant, therefore I couldn't think of anything I needed. He knew I wasn't going to be the fool he thought I was and sped angrily out of my driveway. My words finally rang true!

A few months later, I overheard some of the women in the office talking about the woman in the photograph. She had given birth to a set of twins. Oh, did I pray she'd be a good mother to those twins, and thanked God it wasn't me. I mistakenly had believed that Sid and I were meant to be together in a romantic relationship, but I learned we were meant to be just friends. I had gotten involved with Sid because I was lonely and I enjoyed his, company. His witty humor kept me laughing. He wasn't really a bad soul, but just a young man with a sex drive as big as his ego.

A few months later Sid showed up at a dub where my band was playing. During our break I went over to say hello. He got up and moved to another table when he saw me walking toward him. His behavior caught me off guard. I started to walk away and said to myself, Forget it.

But I was determined to let him know that we were both responsible for using each other. I went to his table and sat do n before he could get up. I said, "Randy, we should at least speak to each other. After all, we were intimate and I'm not the one who cheated and lied." I watched the angry expression on his face begin to soften. He admitted that I was right and apologized to me for the pain he had caused. He told me all about the twins and said he was going to do his best to take care of them. He felt bad because their mother didn't want anything more to do with him.

We unloaded a lot of bad feelings that night and, as a result, became good friends. He knew he could talk to me about all of his problems. I'm glad that I didn't allow my emotions to overrule my good senses, because I wouldn't have been able to grow in understanding or learn the best way to deal with such obstacles in my life.

I was proud of my accomplishments and told him about my new home on Hanna Street. It was an older home in need of repair, but it had a swimming pool! I felt rich with excitement and knew I had won Sid's deepest respect.

Accepting responsibility for my actions is the reason I'm able to forgive. I had convinced myself that a good-looking man with a good job and a new car always has good intentions. I knew it wasn't true, but I wanted what I wanted. Knowing and admitting the truth about my experiences allows me not to suffer. Keeping the blame where it belongs gives me a choice to either stay or go.

Chapter 11

Smoothing Out A Bumpy Road
"Moving Past My Fears"

After several years in Tampa, I began toying with the idea of sneaking back to Philly. I was longing to see my family and friends. Our annual family reunion was scheduled to be in Philadelphia within a few months, so I put on my "brave" wings and booked a flight. My thoughts were so full of excitement that no room had been left for my fears. I was going home!

It was wonderful to see my family, especially my mom and dad. My mother actually gave me a genuine h g! Getting hugs and kisses from my mother had always been a longing in my soul. When I looked into her eyes I saw the love she hadn't been able to express for years. Even though we didn't get to the "I love you" part, I felt it was there.

My father stood by, his head bowed and his han9-s deep into his pockets. I sensed a sickness in his soul over what he had done to me. We had never discussed his unwanted sexual advances toward me, but I could hear regret in his voice whenever I talked with him. I sometimes felt that he blamed himself for my situation. He looked at me with love and fear in his eyes. I knew what he was thinking. Cal was never my dad's favorite person and maybe it was because my father identified with his abusive behavior toward me.

I prayed that time and distance would have softened Cal's heart about coming after me. But I wasn't holding my breath. I'd witnessed firsthand how relentless Cal could be when it came to retrieving what he considered to be "his possession."

At night, when my cousins and I went dubbing, we would hang out in Jersey or on the far side of Philly. We wanted to make sure we wouldn't run into Cal. However, before the week was over, that's exactly what happened.

We stopped at a dub located on a side of town I'd never been to. As soon as we were inside, I felt as if someone was pouring ice down my spine. When looking around for a place to sit, I saw Cal's face and froze. The look on his face indicated he thought he was dreaming. He slowly walked towards me ... my body felt like it was going to dissolve. He got closer and reached inside his jacket pocket ... I pictured myself dead. He pulled out a pack of cigarettes, smiled, and spoke to me. That smile and his voice told me he was no longer in a murderous mood.

He said, "Fate must have caused us to bump into each other because I've never been at this dub before." He said he was glad to see me and asked how I had been.

It took a minute for my voice to materialize and in a whisper I said, "I'm doing fine but I was just leaving."

He asked if I would go by and say hello to his mother because she would love to see me. I promised I would and zoomed past him like a new Thunderbird. I was outta there! I flashed past my cousin so fast it took her a few seconds to collect her thoughts enough to follow me. My heart was pounding so loudly I needed ear plugs.

As she unlocked her car I kept looking back at the club's door to see if Cal was coming after me. I was sure his calm appearance had been only a ploy to throw me off guard. I was so afraid of running into him again that night, I pleaded with my cousin to take me home.

After a few anxious days and a lot of prayers I regained my confidence and enjoyed the remainder of my visit. To be certain that I wouldn't bump into Cal again, my cousins and I would drive the ninety miles to New York for all of our partying.

However, I did take him up on his suggestion to visit his mother. I longed to give her a big hug and tell her how much I missed her. She had been my "sanity" during my insane relationship with her son. Shortly after arriving in Florida I'd contacted her. There was no need to swear her to secrecy; she'd never tell my whereabouts. She knew my reason for leaving her son and strongly supported my decision. We had a wonderful but short visit. I didn't want "fate" to play any more tricks on me.

A year later, I heard from Cal again. He'd persuaded my mom to give him my telephone number, telling her he had important news to tell me. I no longer perceived him as an insane madman, and I guess my mom didn't either. I heard the excitement in his voice as he explained how he had discovered Islam. He was now a Muslim with a new name and a new outlook on life. He apologized to me for the abuse and asked me to accept his friendship.

I held the telephone away from my ear, staring at it, thinking, Either he's got some really good drugs, or he's sincere. Listening to him erased any doubt that he didn't believe in the message that brought life to his dead soul.

The mean snarl was even gone from his voice. He was happy to share his transformation with me. He also suggested I go to my local masjid (church) and listen to the message of Islam. He knew the curiosity I always had about different religions and thought it would be of value to me. I wasn't sure if I was ready to accept advice about what was "good for me" from Cal, but the respect in his voice and his heartfelt apology were enough to convince me that if Islam could change his life, it was definitely something I needed to know about.

I had been exposed to the so-called black Muslims in the early sixties when a friend of mine, Anna, was dating a Muslim brother. We'd sneak across the bridge and listen to the message of Malcolm X and Elijah Mohammad as they spoke from their makeshift pulpit on the street corners of New York. I was impressed with the teachings of the Quran, the sacred writings of Islam, but didn't agree with their concept on race relations. The belief that the white man was "the green-eyed devil" wasn't something I could embrace as being truth from God.

Cal assured me that the new leader, Warith Dean Mohammad, no longer taught that message. I accepted Cal's apology and promised I'd go to the next meeting. Since Islam had such a positive impact on Cal, I knew it could probably help me.

Besides, God's timing couldn't have been better. The desire to become closer to God had prompted me to quit the band and soon I began visiting local churches in search of guidance.

I thought it would be difficult, if not downright impossible, to forgive anyone who had physically abused me and tried every way he could to crush my spirit. But since I had forgiven Sid, I became stronger in the belief I had in myself I realized it was to my advantage to forgive Cal. He was not to blame for my hanging around for so long; that had been my responsibility.

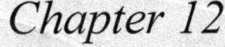

Chapter 12

Navigating Reality
"Embracing the Spirit"

Within a few days I went to my first meeting at the local masjid, and sat there overwhelmed at the teachings of Islam delivered by the new leader by way of radio hookup. This was not the same message I'd heard in the '60s. This was about God, ''Allah" and love, not about race or hatred.

I was also amazed at how much the teachings of the Holy Bible are interwoven with the message of Islam. The Bible reads-in so many words-"You will reap what you sow." Those words were made even more clear to me as the local teacher read a verse from the Quran that went: "We ignore the warnings and follow our own lust, but every matter has its appointed time and every deed must have its inevitable consequences."

I understood the depth of what God meant when he/she breathed those words into the universe. All the questions I'd had about my relationship with God were answered that day. I immediately joined the religion, and legally changed my name from Rosa Lee Peeler to Rose Bilal. Most Africans and American Indians believe a name should mean more than just a fancy sound. It should be something that inspires you to achieve greatness.

I'd read that Bilal was the name of an Ethiopian slave and the first convert to Islam. I admired his independence and courage to claim Islam at a time no one else dared step forward. He was tortured for his refusal to worship idols, but did not yield. He bravely insisted that slaves be treated fairly and justly. I was proud to take his name.

As usual, whenever I accept a responsibility I pour my heart and soul into it. I took on the dress of the Eastern Muslims and began wearing colorful turbans and long flowing dresses. I was so happy with my life that I began to redecorate my home to reflect my inner peace, and contemplated becoming a vegetarian. I did what I believed was right for me. I didn't consider the effect my drastic changes would have on other people, and that was a big mistake.

Evidently my newly found spirituality was causing a lot of concern to the higher-ups at my job. My work evaluations had always been above reproach, so they didn't have grounds to justify firing me. I had no idea they were even entertaining that thought. Although I'd grown tremendously in understanding, I innocently believed as long as I worshiped God, it didn't matter what name I chose to do it under.

My immediate supervisor began to subtly harass me by pretending she couldn't pronounce my name and saying the customers were making fun of the way I dressed. I'd never heard of any customer complaints against me, so I reminded her about the laws regarding religious persecution. Management didn't want to deal with that issue, so they backed off-or so I thought.

One night, the phone mart where I worked was robbed. The next day the police informed us of the burglary as we arrived at work. We were questioned to see if we could provide any information about what happened. Whoever did it had entered with a key, and knew the combination to the safe. All phone mart employees had a key, but only five knew the combination to the safe; and, yes, I was one of those five people.

My co-workers and I spent the rest of that day trying to figure out who could've robbed us. We all wondered, was it really someone in the company? We also feared for our safety because we took in a lot of money, and that meant the thief could be desperate enough, not to get caught, to do some real harm.

A couple days went by with no word on how the investigation was going. After the excitement died, I put the burglary in the back of my mind and focused my thoughts on doing my job.

When I arrived at work on the third day, I was told to report to my supervisor's office. This wasn't unusual and I wasn't concerned, until I saw two white men in dark suits sitting there ... and they were not smiling. One of them said that one of my co-workers had informed them she thought she saw my car at the phone mart on the night of the burglary.

I wondered why she'd say that to them, when she hadn't mentioned it to me, especially since the break,-. In was all we could talk about.

The detectives informed me that everyone had agreed to take a lie detector test and they wondered if I had any objection. I readily agreed. Then my past stopped dead in front of my eyes. My recent life had been so different, I'd almost forgotten. I prayed they couldn't hear what I was thinking. I knew if I refused, .they'd think I was guilty. But a lie detector would reveal everything, including the lie on my application about not having a record. I wanted to disappear!

A union representative happened to come into the phone mart during this time and he interceded. He advised me not to take the lie detector test because not only are they not reliable, they can be used against you. I let out a deep sigh of relief because I knew he was right. My past was safe, at least temporarily.

That afternoon the union rep informed me that no one else had been asked to take the test. Why had the detectives lied? I found out later that they'd acted on advice from someone in upper management. It became clear that management was using this incident to accomplish their mission; now they had a perfect reason to move me from the public's eye. I'd been with GTE long enough to know if they really had believed I'd robbed them, they would have fired me on the spot and never allowed me to continue taking in customer bill payments.

I kept waiting for my immediate supervisor or Mrs. Crawford, the one who spoke so highly of my character, to speak out about what the company was trying to do to me. But I soon realized that the fear of losing their job prevented them from speaking out on my behalf

Once again my friends disappeared in my hour of need. I thought that because they were women they would be more understanding. Even though I was hurt and demoralized, I had to accept that their silence meant they also had families to support. Would I have stood up for them?

The union arranged a meeting for us to try and settle the issue. At the meeting the company alluded to their suspicions, but stopped short of accusing me of the theft. I knew I was being set up and I knew why. All of my hard work and loyalty meant nothing to them. The situation became unbearable. I was being treated unjustly by my company and secretly talked about by my co-workers, who now believed me to be a burglar.

I wanted to commit murder! I realized at that moment how easy it would have been to cross the line. I looked into their lying faces and wondered where I could buy a gun.

I heard a loud voice booming from deep inside of me, saying, NO ONE DESERVES TO DIE BECAUSE OF YOUR ANGER. THINK ABOUT THE FAMILIES OF THE PEOPLE YOU WANT DEAD. THINK ABOUT YOUR FAMILY. GOD WON'T BE PLEASED IF YOU DO THIS. YOU NEED TO DIG DEEP FOR STRENGTH, REACH HIGH FOR FAITH, AND YOU'LL MAKE IT THROUGH THIS.

The voice was right, I knew, but I couldn't calm myself to the point where it made a difference in my thinking. I was shaking so hard that I thought the water was going to spill out of my body.

When the meeting was over I headed straight to the telephone, looked in the yellow pages under Psychiatrist, picked a name, and dialed the number. I tried to explain to the receptionist-who kept' insisting I needed an appoint   When the meeting was over I headed straight to the telephone, looked in the yellow pages under Psychiatrist, picked a name, and dialed the number. I tried to explain to the receptionist-who kept' insisting I needed an appointment-that I was afraid of the murderous thoughts I was having and I needed to talk to the doctor right away. By then I was crying so hard she agreed for me to come in immediately.

I begged the doctor to put me in hospital right away since I was afraid of what I might do; I truly didn't trust my own judgment.

He saw the shape I was in, agreed with me about the need for hospitalization, and explained to me that since I wasn't physically ill, I would have to be put in Charter Hospital, a place that dealt with patients with mental problems. I told him I didn't care; at the time, I was having a mental problem. At the end of the required seventy-two-hour hospital stay, I was still angry enough to pull the trigger, so I begged the doctor for more time. He informed me my insurance would cover up to thirty days. And so I got what I needed.

The depressing fog that had invaded my world allowed me to fit in with the walking zombie patients at Charter. A nurse, who watched to make sure you took them, gave meds twice daily. I quickly learned how to hide the "elephant killing" tranquilizers under my tongue. I didn't want my judgment to be malfunctioning any more than it was.

I had no choice but to return to work at the end of the thirty days. When I arrived at work I found that my position as cashier no longer existed. The exact reason given to me for their decision was "They didn't trust you working with their money." There was no escaping their cruelty. This never-ending nightmare was happening for no other reason than I had chosen a different way to serve God.

I knew I had to demand the justice I deserved, no matter the cost. I contacted a lawyer and told him I wanted to sue.

He said, "You have a good case, but you don't have enough money to go up against the lawyers of a major corporation. They'll tie you up in court for years. And, because you live in the state of Florida and you're a union member, the law wouldn't allow you to go outside of that union to seek representation."

With those words, my heart sank. The last meeting I'd had with the company and the union hadn't gone well. I'd refused to sign their statement implying guilt and wouldn't accept their monetary offer of ten thousand dollars. The union thought the offer was fair and I should have been satisfied. The union rep had gotten angry with me for refusing to sign, and abruptly left the meeting. His action confirmed for me the rumors I'd heard about the company being bought off by the union.

I wanted to take the money and run, but couldn't bring myself to sign a statement that implied I was guilty of committing the burglary. With that kind of stigma I knew I'd never be able to get another job. All negotiations ended at that point.

So, for the next four months, my body continued to perform the robotic routine of my job, but my mind yearned for the freedom I felt in my soul the day I had left Philadelphia. I often thought about my therapy sessions at Charter on managing stressful situations. And because of them I was able to accept the curious stares and questions I experienced from my new co-workers. They couldn't understand why I left the phone mart because everybody wanted to work there. I couldn't answer their questions because I was too embarrassed, and I couldn't bear the thought of nasty rumors swirling around me again.

The more I was forced to endure, the deeper I looked for answers. I later realized that whenever I turned off all outside distractions and deeply questioned my spirit, I found "me"-and I liked her. I thought back on the rocky road of my life and realized not only did I survive the potholes I fell into, but was strong enough to pull myself out, stand up tall, and walk away believing in myself more than ever. I smiled at the thought of this courageous woman I was becoming.

In the mist of all this, my father died from lung cancer. When the doctor told him his condition was .terminal his only comment was "Oh well, I was told twenty-five years ago to stop smoking. I didn't choose to do it and I enjoyed every cigarette I smoked."

Because of his faith and strong belief, I knew he was at peace and in a good place. I can't explain why I didn't resent my father for what he did to me. I knew that alcohol had certainly played a big part. He proved he regretted his actions by his always being there for me. I recall the time he flew to Tampa for the sole purpose of repairing my car. That truly warmed my heart. I so missed his hugs; the ones my mother wasn't able to give me. I'd always admired my father's ability to overcome obstacles. He'd kept himself connected to God, and eventually found the strength he needed to overcome his addiction. He never looked back. I could hear his voice telling me that I had to remove myself from this situation before it ate away at me, like the cancer that had taken his life.

He had said to me, "If you really believe in God like you say you do, then you know everything will be all right no matter what happens, and I will always be there to take care of you." As I stood there reflecting, that same voice said, "Every deed must have its inevitable consequences."

It was then I remembered all the cars I had stolen, and their undeserving victims.

There I was blaming the road and not taking responsibility! And where was my newfound faith? I was mad at myself; I had lied to myself early on and now I was paying for it.

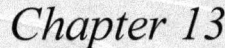

Chapter 13

My Turn Signals Are Working!
"Stepping Out"

Remembering my father's words transformed me from a woman filled with fear and hate, to a woman who was ready to walk on water. On a Monday morning in January of 1989, the "new me" walked into my supervisor's office and informed her, "I quit." She thought I was joking and told to me to sit down because she was too busy to play games.

Finally I convinced her I wasn't joking, and she was too amazed to speak. When her voice returned she said, "You can't just quit, you have to give two weeks' notice."

I assured her that GTE wouldn't have given me the courtesy of a two weeks' notice had they fired me. I said, "If the company needs a notice, then take what I'm telling you now and make it retroactive because I'm out of here." I handed her my I.D. badge and left the building. As I drove out of the parking lot, I experienced a brief moment of panic. "I've just quit my job and I don't have any money!", my brain screamed loudly to me.

Visions of Robert and Penny crying thunderstorm tears danced by my eyes. After the death of my father, I'd taken on the responsibility of helping my mother financially to raise my niece and nephew. Robert and Penny were good children who knew they could count on me, and I didn't want to let them down. Fear almost caused me to go back and beg for my job; but after a few moments I became calm. I knew I had done the right thing. I had no chance of climbing the ladder with a company I knew wanted to push me off. They would've found another reason to persecute me.

Whenever I'm in need of an extra helping of courage, I think back to a young man I once saw lying in his hospital room, who was paralyzed from his neck down. His eyes were the only things he had control 0£ They were wide with fear and frustration as they followed a big black fly around the room that was headed straight for his nose. As the nurse gently shooed away the fly, I reflected on how

much we take for granted and how insignificant my problems were. I'm sure that man would have gladly traded places with me.

I suddenly recognized the healthy energy surging through my body, and knew that I was able to reach out to my world and touch it. I could feel the grass between my toes. Man, that was a fabulous gift! Besides, I knew I'd be okay; my father told me so.

It felt odd not having to get up early and go to work the next day. I decided not to tell my mother I was unemployed until I knew what I was going to do. I spent the entire day in a gray cloud mood, trying to figure out my next move. I'd only three thousand dollars left from the eight thousand dollars in my savings. I had used most of it to bury my father and support my mother until she received his Social Security benefits. I had to accept the fact that I would probably lose my house, new truck, and excellent credit rating. That didn't cause me too much concern because I knew I could have it all again. I'd left behind more than that when I made my escape from Philadelphia.

I was helped by the financial support of my family and the few good friends who still believed in me. It was comforting to know that my family loved me, even the ones who were no longer physically present.

When news got out that I'd quit my job, my telephone rang off the hook. My co-workers were calling to say I was crazy to walk away from my "good-paying" job.

Without knowing all the facts of the situation, it was difficult for anyone to understand my actions. I dreaded the disappointment I knew I'd hear in my mother's voice when I told her that I had quit.

I was warmly surprised at my mother's supportive response. Even though my mother understood the reason for my drastic decision, she was concerned about how we would make it. I knew by her unasked questions that she secretly thought I'd lost my mind. How could I possibly help pay for Robert's college education now, or keep the roof over our heads? To calm her fears I convinced her I had a solid plan to take care of them and myself. Of course, I was bluffing!

I've never been afraid of hard work, and was prepared to do whatever I could legally to survive. Even if it meant following in my mother's footsteps and doing domestic work. I respected her and all the women who had come before her. My mother had been forced, by the absence of finances, to take nothing and turn it into the food and staples that held a family together. Pride was not an issue for me, and I had a sense of peace in knowing I was a survivor. I knew that if I went inside of myself and looked for the answers I needed, they would let me find them. The only thing I knew to do as ... keep on praying.

My prayers were answered. I got the answer I had been looking for when a girlfriend of mine suggested I open a consignment shop. I'd never heard of consignment, but became interested when I learned that the customers provided the inventory. They would bring their "mint condition" wearing apparel and received fifty percent commission when the items sold. It sounded to me like an upscale version of a thrift store. I could relate to that. I took the last $2,000 I had left and invested it in a store I found available in a lower-income section of town. Since it was on the corner, I thought the location was good. The rent was an affordable $200 a month, which made it possible for me to open Bilal's Consignment Shop.

The bank eventually foreclosed on my house, and my only alternative was to convert the rear of my store into an apartment, which I moved into. I was only there a week before my mom sent Robert and Penny to live with me for a while. She was planning on eventually moving to Florida and needed time to put things in order. I now think that was her way of teaching me how to make something out of nothing. Two young and impressionable people were depending on me.

Penny and I added a "woman's touch" to my homemade apartment: curtains here, a plant there, and soon we made it comfortable for us all. They were enrolled at Hillsborough High and accepted fondly by their peers. Robert, a teenager, made good grades in school and dreamed of going to West Point. Patricia, called Penny, only wanted to get through high school. She'd fallen in love with a classmate, Michael, and saw only marriage in her future. I wanted to set a good example for Robert and Penny, which forced me to keep things going.

Once again I was embraced by fear when my money began to run out and I wasn't making enough to replace it. Fear is sometimes like a roadblock; it will keep you from finding your faith and cause you to detour from your morals. One evening, after dosing my store, I went to a local supermarket where I had once worked part-time as a cashier. In the checkout line, I realized I didn't have enough money to pay for the food I had in my cart. I convinced myself that I would be justified if I put a few of the items in my purse. After all, I thought they hadn't paid me a decent wage when I was employed there, so they owed me the food.

This was a time when I should have been applying the brakes! Mr. Davis, the store manager, watched on his surveillance camera. Thank God I only took three lemons. He walked me to the break room in the back of the store and told me he had seen what I had done. As I sat ther more ashamed than I'd ever been in my life, he said, "Rose, I like you and I'm not going to have you arrested, but you are no longer welcome to shop at this store."

I felt the self-disgust I should have felt when I was stealing cars. It was amazing; I thought I had left that part of me in Philadelphia. I prayed that Robert and Penny would never find out what was taking me so long to get back. The shame burned through me worse than any physical pain, and I vowed to never let fear put me in that position again.

It dosen't matter if it's a lemon or a car; stealing can never be justified. There's always another way.

Chapter 14

Nearing My Destination
"Rose Blossoms"

After a few months without customers, I knew I needed help. Then something happened that was so out of the ordinary I knew it came from the spiritual presence of my dad. A medium-built man entered my store and introduced himself as Ogun Tolu. He said someone told him that my store might be a good place for him to sell his hand-made beads and wood sculptures. He was adorned from head to toe in full African dress that complemented his caramel-colored complexion. I was curious about his dress and he gently explained that it was called a "grand buba," worn only by men of stature. The poncho-shaped garment shone with the colors of a blazing African sun. I was impressed with his artwork, and knew I'd have no problem selling it, if only I could get the customers.

When I told him how I wasn't having any luck in getting sales, he parted his lips in a big smile, and through ivory white teeth said, "Then you need to talk to my wife. Her name is Majile Osun Bunmi. In fact, we are having a party tonight and I know Bunmi would love it if you came." He wrote down his address and said, "My wife has been an African priestess for years, and I know her readings will help you."

I had no idea what he meant by "readings," but felt I had to go to his party. I filled out a receipt for his sculptures and, before he left, I told him I'd consider the offer.

Shortly before quitting the phone company, I'd started smoking cigarettes. I took a long hard pull on the Benson & Hedges menthol between my lips and tried to figure out if I owned anything that looked ethnic enough to wear to their party. The grand dress of Tolu had awakened my ethic curiosity. I felt the need to wear something that represented my roots. I'd smoked at least three cigarettes before remembering that I'd been given a beautiful African print blouse as a birthday gift.

I felt comfortable at the social event that evening, which consisted of their immediate family and a few intimate friends. Bunmi was a beautiful pecan-tan woman that fit every image I'd ever had of an African queen. Her elegant posture implied she came from a long line of royalty. Her dark brown eyes were wise and so compelling, I felt as if she could see into my soul. She said she was a priestess in the worship of Orisha. This religious belief has survived successfully throughout Africa and especially among the Yoruba tribe of present-day Nigeria for over 5,000 years. It is nonjudgmental in character, therefore avoiding the traps of ethical religious systems, many of which produce guilt.

Throughout the evening, the conversations ranged from African spiritual beliefs to local community issues. Bunmi was dearly respected as leader and head of the family, and I was impressed with how informed and concerned they all were about the poor economic condition of African American people. I realized I knew next to nothing about my African origin and had taken it for granted that my ancestors had only been slaves.

The belief system of my parents and most of the people I knew, gave me the impression that black people were nothing more than servants and the color of our skin was something to be ashamed of. Years later, my father told me he'd always been too embarrassed to talk with me about pride, because of the indignity he felt from the treatment he was forced to endure. I wondered if that had been the motivating force behind his injuring other souls. Was this his way of feeling superior? Most white people assumed because he was uneducated he was stupid. But the reality was that he'd had to quit school to support his mother. His soul was bruised as he watched uneducated white men being promoted. There were times when he had to fight with himself not to hate all white people. He knew they weren't all racist. He used to say, "Colored folks would still be slaves if some white folks hadn't believed it was wrong."

As I listened to Bunmi talk about Africa's beauty and rich history,

I knew I had finally escaped from the slavery of ignorance. I could hardly wait to share this knowledge with Robert and Penny. I knew the impact it could have on their young lives. By the end of the evening I felt a kinship to Bumni's family and friends. She said she was pleased to have met me, and scheduled a 10 a.m. appointment the very next morning for our reading session.

In my shower the next morning, I felt the sensation of two hands being cupped around my left ear, and I heard my father say, in a dear voice, "You'd better put those cigarettes down!" I bolted from the shower and ran for the front door. Thank God I was there alone. I was shocked out of my lunatic moment when I flung open the back door and felt the assaulting morning air attack my naked body. I was shaken to the bone, but managed to calm my fears enough to keep my appointment.

Bunmi greeted me with a puzzled look on her face. "Do you smoke cigarettes," she asked. I'd deliberately not smoked at her party and wondered why she'd ask that question. She said she'd heard a voice that morning who said he was a dose ancestor of mine, and he wanted her to tell me to stop smoking. The voice said he had tried to get through to me, but I had been too frightened to listen. I immediately tried to figure out where she had hidden the microphone. How else could she know about the spooky episode with my father, or that I smoked. I thought about my mother saying, "There are people who will put 'roots' or 'spells' on you." I had to get outta there.

Bunmi saw my eyes searching for an exit and told me not to be afraid. She said, "My role is to teach and to heal, not to hurt you."

She told me that I should honor the wishes of my ancestors, because their only purpose is to protect and guide their loved ones throughout their existence. It is the belief of Orisha that it is your birthright to be happy, successful, and fulfilled. The spirit of our ancestors does exist and must be honored. I'd always heard voices and felt the presence of the spirits around me; but I understood it to mean that I might need psychiatric help.

Now it all made sense. I had to learn to trust the voices that talk to my soul because they would guide me through the difficulties I'd encounter on my journey through life. Even though I still had some concerns, I sat down for my reading.

The divination used by Bunmi in order to make connection with the spiritual energy of my ancestors was sixteen cowrie shells.

She placed the shells in the palms of her hands, and then touched them to the center of my forehead, both of my shoulders, and the palms of my hands. Then she threw them like dice, and the formation in which they fell gave Bunmi the information she read to me.

She said, "The spirits around you are very strong. They want you to know they are there to help you fulfill your dreams. God has opened your heart to accept the mysteries of the universe and to worship your ancestors."

I don't know if I believed everything Bunmi told me that day, but I felt as if I had a new power guiding me on my road to success. Bunmi told me the shells had revealed that I was worried about losing my store, but I was not to worry because everything would be fine. I thought to myself, Ha! I knew those silly shells were no good, or else she would have known about the eviction notice I'd gotten the day before. I cunningly displayed a "thanks for nothing" smile on my face as I thanked her for my reading and left.

The bewildered voice of my landlord on the phone the next morning snapped me to attention: "I've had a change of heart," she said. "I'm dropping the eviction and wiping out all your back debts. An angel appeared to me in my dream and told me to give you more time."

That was only the beginning of many phenomenal occurrences that keep showing up in my life. Shortly after my reading with Bunmi, a woman visited my store. She was a reporter for' the Tampa Tribune, a local newspaper. She was working on an article about the accomplishments of minorities and asked if she could include me. I could see my dad smiling! Thanks to the article about my being the only black woman in Tampa operating a consignment shop, my business picked up a little, and it allowed me to stay in business for another year, before finally having to close. I'd stepped out on faith, and in my ignorance I almost made it work. But my skills were now leading me in another direction.

My financial picture was getting dimmer, and looming on the horizon was the fact of my having to get a job. However, I had no intention of returning to the corporate world.

I asked God and my ancestors to help me stretch my meager savings a little while longer. At least until Robert and Penny were gone. My prayerful stare was aimed at the wall while I pleaded for guidance. As my consciousness returned I was mindful of my surroundings.

I hadn't tried to draw anything since grade school, but I needed to brighten the bare walls in my store. I had the idea to paint figures of trapeze artists swinging toward the ceiling. Wanting something even more colorful, I painted a pudgy clown with a banana yellow straw hat, a purple polka-dot shirt, crimson- striped pants, and big floppy black shoes. I had a lot of fun expressing my creative self again, but knew I was no Van Gogh.

A customer visiting the store was impressed with the clown and wanted to commission a life-size version of it on a canvas. I was all set to explain to her that I wasn't a real artist when she said, "I would be willing to pay whatever you want-I'll even buy your supplies."

I readily agreed to do the painting! It was then I realized that my artwork could possibly be a way for me to make a living. Not having a clue how to paint anything on canvas forced me to stall for time. Words started coming at me so fast and loud, I thought at first they were coming from my customer. Words like "Don't you go thinkin' you ain't no artist," "We done sent you a way to make some money," "All you got to do is tell yourself you can do it, and you gon make it happen." The louder the voices got, the stronger I felt because I knew they were coming from my ancestors.

I asked for her name and phone number and told her that as soon as I got the prices for supplies, I'd get back to her. After she left the store, I ran to the yellow pages and walked my fingers to "art supplies," eventually calling Pearl Art Store. From a helpful clerk I got the information about what supplies I would need, and began imagining how I'd draw a happy dancing down with a fiery red nose.

Later that night when I went to pick up my supplies, I noticed a fine-looking, light-skinned black man hanging around the counter listening in on the questions I asked the salesclerk. He reminded me of a college student, in his casual dress of jeans and open-collared white shirt. It was a liberating feeling to admire a man and not have to wonder if he's the one who's going to "make me happy."

I must have unconsciously been staring at him because I noticed him looking back at me. At first I thought he was trying to flirt, then he came over and introduced himself. He said his name was Oliver Parsons and that he had recently assembled a group of local artists whose mission was to produce artwork for sale. His sales pitch helped me understand how the hands-on instruction from other artists would benefit me if I joined their group. I took a quick look toward the sky and silently thanked God and my ancestors for steering me to this particular art store.

I met the other members of the group at their Sunday weekly meeting and immediately found them to be very warm and helpful. I bombarded them with so many questions I was afraid they were going to start charging for their services. Instead they patiently showed me how to travel the road of art. I began to learn all the techniques of mixing colors and what brushes to use; and, in no time, I had painted a beautiful down on a five-foot canvas and was paid my asking fee of $600. Without the benefit of formal training I had become an accomplished painter. I was a real artist! My niece and nephew didn't know what to make of their "brush stroking" auntie.

It seemed as if these skills had been stored up, waiting for me to find the freedom and courage to apply them. Once I learned the concept of shadow and light, I never wanted to stop painting. I painted every picture I saw on magazine covers from TV Guide to Vogue. I learned more about anatomy by studying the faces and poses in my old family photos. In some way, it helped me bring my memories of them into my work-the passion and the pain. My eye for detail was getting sharper and I was starting to develop my own style.

A year later, while I was painting a mural on the window of the Blues Ship nightclub in Ybor City, Tampa's Latin quarter, Malcolm Johnson, a local art connoisseur from St. Petersburg, noticed me and asked if he could nominate me for the public arts program there. Since I never thought I'd be commissioned, I agreed.

When I found out I would be competing against fifteen professional artists, I experienced a brief moment of panic. After all, they had all been to art school and had degrees. We had been asked to make a presentation in front of a selected panel from the St. Petersburg Arts Council. I thought, What have I gotten myself into! But before my fear went into overdrive, I won the competition.

I was so excited that I called everybody I knew, including my garage mechanic, and told them I had been hired by the city of St. Petersburg to paint a mural on a three-story building.

I'd never attempted anything of that magnitude, and fear almost caused me to turn it down. I reminded myself of the obstacles I'd already overcome and decided this wasn't going to be my stop sign. I remembered admiring a large mural of an American eagle painted on a two-story brick building in downtown Tampa. The artist had signed his name and added his telephone number on the finished mural. I called the artist, Ron Berman, and told him of my dilemma. I offered him pay and begged him to show me how he had painted the mural. He agreed to help me for nothing more than the price of lunch.

We met the next day and, in no time at all, Ron taught me how to scale up an 8 x 10 painting to fit a three-story building and what supplies were needed. He shared my intense desire to be creative and asked if I'd like to work with him, to learn more about murals. I leapt at the opportunity. Ron's wife and secretary was Diane. I'm certain she's the reason his work has such deep expressions of love. Ron had been getting a lot of local attention for his imaginative artwork. I felt lucky to have met such a talented artist willing to share his secrets with me. I'm sure my ancestors had a hand in pointing my paintbrush in Ron's direction. I'm even more convinced they gave me the idea of what I would be painting on my building.

With the city paying for everything including the rental of the scaffolding, I painted "Jubilation," a picture of five African women dancing in bright red, green, and yellow dresses. Overcoming my fear of heights and gaining the courage to climb up on three stories of scaffolding was enough to convince me that I could accomplish anything I set out to do. I felt as if my spirit had eaten all of Popeye's spinach and I now had enough strength to lift the universe.

Every time I overcame my fears, it helped to strengthen my belief in something outside of me. A year after I left my job I stopped

wearing my turbans and long dresses. I came to believe that my connection to God or the universe has nothing to do with which religion I belong to, or how I dress. I think what Jesus was trying to teach us in his message of love, is tolerance. If we can't tolerate the differences of our mates or other people, we will never learn to love them and we will blame them for our unhappiness or lack of success.

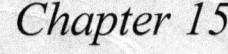

Chapter 15

Smooth Road Ahead
"Straighter and Stronger"

Weeding the soil of my negative thoughts and fears allowed my creative energy to blossom. Seeing a papier-mâché exhibit at a local art gallery turned me into a newspaper-collecting fool. I tried desperately to duplicate the lifelike sculptures captured so eloquently by the artist. I experimented every way I could think of, hoping to reproduce those amazing images.

In 1997, I created a formula for ...turning newspaper into a consistency that allows me to sculpt with it as if I was using day. Blending together newspaper and glue into a pancake-like consistency made it possible for me to shape intricate facial features such as noses. I was even able to sculpt teeth and fingernails. When it came to designing the clothes for my dolls, I used the sewing skills I'd acquired during my prison stay. Wanting my dolls' hair to be as unique as their outfits caused me to dig out my old wigs and create hairstyles to match their character. I braided and pony-tailed myself silly. I decided to call the figures I created, "Paper Girls. I'd finally begun playing with dolls!"

Fellow artists encouraged me to try and get my captivating dolls entered into the local annual art show. Not only would my sculptures attain the exposure they needed, I could also make money. I submitted the required four slides of my latest work to the Brandon League of Fine Arts, and was accepted as a participant in the upcoming show.

I used up every minute in the four months prior to the show building my dolls. They gave the appearance of having an afternoon tea party when I sat them on the lawn to dry in the sun. I worked on several at once. I asked the spirit of the late fashion designer, Edith Head, to guide my elaborate creations. She answered my humble prayer. My gowns turned out fabulous. In order to capture the attitude of "today's woman," I decided to put men's pants on some of the figures.

I won the First Place blue ribbon and a $500 cash award in the first art show I entered. The judges had chosen the sculpture "Sticking with Fosse." My love for the theater and admiration of Bob Fosse, the master choreographer, was my inspiration for that particular work It featured a sculpted woman with long supple legs draped over a high-backed stool. Her smoky eyes focused on the audience. Using both hands she leaned on a black, white-tipped walking stick which accentuated a black pin-striped tuxedo and a shiny top hat cocked to the right side of her head. The tails of her tuxedo hung over the stool, conveying the attitude "I got it made on Broadway!" Her powerful stance seemed to speak to me of the power that I was waking up in myself.

Bunmi told me that I had the eye when it came to art. She said my readings had revealed great things for me in the arts. She right away commissioned me to sculpt a special piece for her ancestral altar. She said, "I better order now because I won't be able to afford you once the word gets out."

During the six-month process of sculpting Oshun, a Yoruba deity representing Love, I realized the confidence and independence that I had developed in becoming a proud woman was being displayed through the women I created out of papier-mâché. I seemed to always give a sense of strength to the formation and movement of the pieces. I envisioned them running, dancing, walking, or standing with an assurance that says, "Yes I can."

It felt great to have people love my sculptures enough to pay money for them. My work was noticed and displayed by art galleries in Kentucky, Georgia, and Florida. Unfortunately, the sale of artwork wasn't something that happened every day, and it wasn't sufficient money to live on.

Looking for another way to make money creatively, I decided to sing again. Robert and Penny, my nephew and niece, were finally on their own, so I had more freedom. Jazz music wasn't something I'd enjoyed listening to when I was younger, and I never dreamed I'd want to sing it. But while listening to the radio in my store one day, the sound of jazz captured me. I'm not sure if it was sounding different to me because I was older, or what; but I loved it and knew I had to sing it.

I started going to the local jazz clubs and making friends with the musicians. The guys at the jam sessions agreed they liked my style and manner of phrasing. They advised me to learn lyrics to some of the old jazz standards and come sit in with them.

The entire week, I listened to the jazz cassettes of Sarah Vaughan, Ella Fitzgerald, Billie Holiday, and Carmen McRae. I learned only the songs I thought fit my style. After a few :weeks I was ready to rev my engine.

Since I was an experienced singer I thought it would be easy to sing jazz, but I quickly learned that the count and timing were quite different than rhythm and blues. I didn't know where to come in singing after the musicians had taken their solos. I prayed the audience wouldn't see me panic whenever I lost my way.

After a few nights of those embarrassing moments, the guys taught me the formula for understanding the A-section and B? section of a song. That information helped take me from zero to sixty on the musical highway.

After a few years of perfecting my presentation, it was time to start booking myself as a "jazz vocalist." The bass player, Mark Neuenschwander, had formed his own jazz combo consisting of piano, bass and drums, and hired me as their vocalist. I began working four nights a week at the "internationally known" Hurricane Lounge in Pass-a-Grille, Florida. The guys in the band voluntarily gave time normally used for "chasing ladies" to rehearse with me. I was able to build one hell of a musical repertoire. Thanks, guys!

One Saturday night while I was singing, a young black man carrying a horn case walked up to Mark and whispered something in his ear. The next thing I knew, that same man took out his trombone and began to accompany me. A few minutes later, another bass player and drummer came up and soon replaced my group, who gratefully gave up their instruments.

When the set was over, I learned that these very talented men were a part of the Wynton Marsalis band who were in town performing at the Ruth Eckerd Hall in Clearwater. I couldn't believe it. These world-famous musicians wanted to play for me! I had to struggle to keep my head from filling the room and my shoes from taking off like rockets! Had I known their identity, my heart would've been beating so loud I wouldn't have heard my cue. My only regret was I didn't have a camera. But Wycliff, the trombone player, did give me his card and told me to call him if ever I needed a horn player. I knew he'd forget my name as soon as he left town, but it felt good to know he thought it an honor to accompany me. Confidence builders like these kept boosting me through the roof! Just when I thought all my talents had surfaced, I was zapped by the acting bug. My acting until then had been limited to one-act shows Bunmi had written for our Kwanzaa celebration. The sensitive issues of her plays both educated and astounded the awestruck audience. Bunmi was a talented director who knew how to draw out my hidden abilities, and in so doing revealed a talent that was to allow me to shift to yet another gear.

The need to act again tugged at my heart during a benefit performance at a local theater. When my band and I took a break, I made arrangements with Anna Brennen, the founder and producing director of Stageworks Theatre Company, to trade my artistic talent for acting classes. I'd heard they needed someone to paint their sets; so we traded.

Anna said I was a natural at acting and wanted to direct me on how to play the characters of historic African American women such as Rosa Parks, Madam C. J. Walker, and ,Mary McLeod Bethune. The performances were to be held at local schools and Boys and Girls Clubs.

Within six months I made my first major stage appearance in a musical written by Trish Gullett, titled "Sing Me, Dance Me." I met Trish through Anna and we'd become good friends. She'd been looking for someone to play the part of her alter-ego and thought I'd do a good job with the role.

During the two weeks of rehearsal, Murphy's Law was operating in full swing. The local sewers overflowed and the theater w filled with a stench beyond description. We used every deodorizer on the market to make the air breathable. As a result, everyone was extra nervous on opening night, but when the curtain fell at the end of the show, we knew it was a hit!

The idea to use my acting ability to try to overcome my stage fright jumped on me one night during one of my gigs. When introduced, I swept gracefully onstage-the way I imagined Nancy Wilson would have done it. I announced the name of the song and then snapped my fingers to count it off-the way I'd seen professional singers do it. After that I pretended to be a famous jazz singer every time I got onstage. Acting out my "self-written" scripts helped me send stage fright speeding out of my life. My jazz shows are now worthy of Carnegie Hall. I thought to myself, Wow, what a great tool! I'll use it whenever I need to steer around the frightening curves of life.

Chapter 16

Bless The Road
"Life in Full Bloom"

L***ocal*** booking agents noticed my natural acting ability. I began to get steady work in jazz dubs and the theater. In 1998 I was hired by a company named School Is Fun Productions, to travel to Alabama, Georgia, and throughout the state of Florida, performing one-woman shows about Harriet Tubman at elementary, middle, and high schools. I continue to this day doing this gratifying work.

Most of the children I perform for are white and have never heard of the characters I portray. I'm grateful that acting allows me the opportunity to tell the stories of these remarkable African Americans. Researching the rich heritage of my ancestry helped erase the shame I was made to feel about the color of my skin. Every time I tell the children of the many contributions made by African Americans, it increases my pride as a black woman. I believe my ancestors use the light from the candles I burn for them to guide me on my path to good fortune.

John Lennon's song, "Instant Karma," was never a favorite of mine. But the first time I had my car stolen, that tune popped right into my head. I was self-righteously cussing out the thieves who had stolen my car, when the white candle on my ancestors' altar caught my eye. At that moment the voice deep inside my soul shouted out to me, Now you know what it feels like. My karma wasn't instant but I eventually got the message. I can truly say I feel as if I've paid that debt. And you know, it feels really good to have that recognition now.

When I think back on the pain I felt in my soul when I was forced to quit my job, it's hard to believe the only thing I feel now is gratitude.

I like what Albert Einstein once said: "It is not possible to solve a problem within the same consciousness that produced it." Amen to that! Had I acted out my selfish thoughts of revenge, I'd never have discovered the beautiful butterfly that was embedded deep in my cocoon of fear. I now know every challenge is a chance to grow and to learn valuable spirit strengthening lessons.

All of the mischief and bad decisions I'd thrown out into the universe hit me with the force of a hundred hurricanes. I survived only because I listened to the voice in the wind that said, "You won't be blown off the path as long as you follow the source that created me."

It would have been easy for me to continue blaming my mother, GTE, and "unfulfilled" relationships for my hurt and pain-most of which I'd caused myself Even worse, I could have taken yet another wrong turn by refusing to even see my faults. That truly would've dimmed the headlights shining down the road to my success.

I love being an actress, vocalist, artist, speaker, and author; and what's even better, I get paid to do what I love. I'm one lucky lady! In fact, sometimes I almost want to send the phone company a thank-you card. If I were still working for them, I wouldn't have had time to discover me. Their actions created the door I was able to walk through to discover my real purpose.

Everything in my life now is rewarding. Having learned the importance of unconditional love, I've remained friends with former partners and wish only the best for them. I now have a wonderful soul mate to cruise life's highway with. His strong spirit, understanding of life, and artistic creative mind allow us the freedom to have a loving, giving relationship. Knowing I'm in control of my happiness permits me the freedom to love without worry. I don't fear the breakup of my relationship because I know I'm always loved. God loves me and I love myself.

But the greatest reward of all is the love I receive from my adult nephew and niece. Their heartfelt Mother's Day and birthday cards let me know how wrong I was in believing I'd make a "lousy mother." One of the best things I've done in my life was being a mother to Robert and Penny. Mentoring them and guiding their lives helped teach me the unconditional love I needed in order to be happy and to grow spiritually. I learned to chip away at the concrete of my soul before it hardened and I became strong enough to love without fear of losing.

Robert didn't get into West Point, but he has managed to work his way up in rank in the Air Force. He was passionate about the military and vowed to stay until retirement. However, fate dealt an ugly blow when after only eleven years he was forced to retire due to personal illness. His marriage also ended, yet he remains dose to his ex-wife, Grace, and their daughter Vanessa.

Penny married her high school sweetheart, Mike. I thought they were too young to make a marriage work, but they've proven me wrong. They recently celebrated their twenty-third wedding anniversary. Their two sons, Michael and Sheldon, have given them five lovely grandchildren.

I hadn't realized the extent my mother's inability to love had affected my life until Penny made me see it. I don't remember the exact words of the quote but it goes: "Wisdom comes from the mouths of babes." She recognized my struggle for identity because of the few short years she'd spent with her mother. My sister Annette worked hard to be a loving mother to Penny and Robert. Their lives are proof of her efforts. Penny says she knows change is not an easy thing to do, but it's necessary and it will only benefit me. She has played a huge role in my development as a parent. She reminds me so much of my sister. She could have been a mother to us both!

Penny shares her innermost concerns with me about the necessary changes in my personality in order for me to be more loving and giving. Things like patience and compassion. I have to admit she's a connoisseur of them both. She deeply loves her brother Robert, and takes very good care of him. Robert tells anyone who'll listen how grateful he is to have Penny as his sister. Her appreciated honesty in our conversations about why we should love each other is paying off. My heart has grown as deep as Dr. Martin Luther King's Sunday sermons. I completely enjoy all the hugs and kisses I get from my great-grandchildren. And they truly are great kids!

However, in the mist of my daydreaming moments, I find myself wishing that my mother and I would somehow reach that same level of intimacy. But we can't find the map to lead us down that road. Recently my mother became ill with high blood pressure and was prescribed several kinds of medication. The circumstances of her illness resulted in my becoming her temporary caregiver. Because of recent memory lapses she was afraid she wouldn't remember to take the pills. Her fear forced her decision to move into an assisted living facility to get the help she needed. Because of her age-well into her eighties-it fell to me to make the arrangements. I could tell my mother wasn't comfortable with my being in charge of her.

Having to gather personal medical data for the nurses helped open the door for other questions. I tried to slip them in as if they were a part of the required information. Questions such as, What's the real reason you married my father? Why is it so hard to show love for me? I felt that talking about those painful issues would help us to get past the barrier between us. She shared with me the hardship of raising a family, but became tightlipped and defensive when I probed into the loveless relationship she shared with my father.

It's unfortunate that my mother is so immovably rooted in her idea that to admit mistakes would mean she'd be judged, never forgiven, and the shame would be too great for her to bear. She doesn't understand that truth is the only way she'll ever outgrow her fears. The more I experience my life, the greater is the appreciation I have for the job she's done-considering her life's unfair working schedule.

I'll always love my mother. Above all, she's given me her strong will of survival. She's provided my soul with the food of life that will nourish my mind through its maze of ignorance.

On February 2, 1997, I had the honor of appearing in a program with world-renowned author Neale Donald Walsch (Conversations with God). He was the guest speaker at The Center of Conscious Living and I sang the opening song, "Our Love Is Here To Stay." At the end of the program, Mr. Walsch presented me with a signed copy of his book. On the inside cover, he'd drawn a caricature of himself, along with a note that read, "To my wonderful Rose!! Thank you for the beautiful gift you are ! Hugs." The light from my soul had been shining so bright that day he couldn't help but notice.

I believe I'm being led by my spirit to share the wisdom I've acquired in my search for the true meaning of love. I believe God doesn't care what names we call our religions or any of the dogma and rituals we hold sacred. What really matters to God is that we love him, respect our families and our ancestors, and live our lives with dignity and integrity. And when we pass those values on to our children by example and not only by words, we send our love back to the God who created us. With all the wisdom I've gained, I've learned to take responsibility for my choices and I will never, ever again blame the road.

Rose Bilal
About the Author

Rose Bilal lived a life of crime, fame and fortune. From the streets of New Jersey and Philadelphia to the big stage as a highly sought after performer. Rose moved to Tampa, Florida in 1969 and expanded her career as a jazz singer, visual artist, motivational speaker and actor. She motivated women and young girls to escellence by sharing her journey touring with "Powerstories".

In her second published book, "A Stroke Saved My Life" Rose details how the stroke she suffered in 2013, altered everything, even her soul.

Rose lives in Tampa with her husband "Chico" and is still on a mission to inspire women to live a great life.

www.ingramcontent.com/pod-product-compliance
Lightning Source LLC
Chambersburg PA
CBHW070906080526
44589CB00013B/1195